SUCCESS

Before You Continue

This book is only the beginning. As a reader of this book, you are entitled to two free bonuses.

Bonus #1:

There is more available free to readers of this book at www.ChuckRylant.com. As a VIP member you will receive brand-new interviews and other inspiring articles immediately as they are published.

Bonus #2:

Readers are also eligible to receive a one-year complimentary subscription to the print newsletter **Extraordinary Living,** which is shipped via USPS to your home or office. To receive your one-year complimentary subscription visit www.ChuckRylant.com/news.

Visit www.ChuckRylant.com and www.ChuckRylant.com/news before you get distracted.

SUCCESS

The Path to Personal Fulfillment Through Brazilian Jiu-Jitsu Fighters

CHUCK J. RYLANT

ISBN-10: 0-9839637-5-4
ISBN-13: 978-0-9839637-5-2

Published by:
Perfect Life Publishing
793 Foothill Boulevard, Suite 165
San Luis Obispo, CA 93405-1683

Cover and Interior Design:
Jerry & Michelle Dorris
Authorsupport.com

Contents

Introduction

This book is a collection of intimate and sometimes shocking conversations about success. Each story will inspire, enlighten, and entertain you.

If you enjoyed the first book, *Motivation: Stories on Life and Success from Brazilian Jiu-Jitsu Black Belts*, then you will absolutely love *Success*. This book follows a format similar to that of *Motivation*, but *Success* goes much deeper.

In *Success*, not only did I seek to discover what motivates high achievers, but I also dug for the philosophies that lead to success.

During these interviews, I asked uncomfortable questions that led to answers that often surprised even the athletes being interviewed, because it is the subconscious mind that drives most ambitious people to achieve.

Each athlete came from a diverse background, but there were common themes that every reader can embrace and model in their own lives. A key takeaway was how each fighter defined success—often their answers contradicted societal norms.

Jiu-Jitsu has often been used as a metaphor for life, but in these stories, you can replace Jiu-Jitsu with any ambitious pursuit—the lessons are universal.

If you're ready to experience an intense journey, let's get started.

Chris Lovato

"I paid 50 bucks for a self-defense seminar," Chris Lovato said, "and all I remember were the takedowns and the instructor doing this weird breathing thing."

At the end of the seminar, the instructor lined the students up and each was given a chance to knock him down.

"I've got this," Chris thought because of his wrestling background. "I jumped to the front of the line and the next thing I knew I was looking up at the ceiling."

Everyone was given one shot, but Chris snuck back in line to try again.

"He got lucky," Chris thought. "I didn't know what the hell happened the second time, but I ended up on my back staring up at the ceiling again. I had no idea who he was, but he fucked me up."

That was Chris's introduction to Brazilian Jiu-Jitsu, and the instructor—Rickson Gracie—was one of the best fighters of all time.

Since then, Chris has gone on to earn black belts in Judo and

Jiu-Jitsu and also owns three Paragon Brazilian Jiu-Jitsu (BJJ) academies. He also serves as the only civilian self-defense instructor at the local police academy and he is a California P.O.S.T. Master Instructor who teaches other police trainers throughout the state of California.

When he started at that first BJJ seminar, Chris had already been wrestling since his junior year of high school in Santa Cruz, California.

"I wasn't terribly good at wrestling, but I really liked it," Chris said. "I got pummeled in my first match and lost by a bunch of points, but I got to cross-face this dude like crazy, and afterwards, the guy was bleeding all over his face. It was the best thing I had ever done because they let me fight, and they actually encouraged it."

Chris got into a lot of fights when he was younger, especially before he had wrestling as an outlet.

"I was bullied a lot," Chris said. "I was scared back then because after school they would gang up on me, shove me against the wall, and beat me."

When Chris got to the eighth grade, he started fighting back.

"I'd finally had enough," Chris said. "I decided that if I was going to get hit, I might as well hit back. One day the leader had my arms pinned against the wall and I didn't know what to do, so I head-butted him in the nose."

When Chris started standing up to his tormentors, people started leaving him alone. He didn't realize it at the time, but the more he fought back, the more empowered he became.

"I realized I could take care of myself," Chris said. "I started getting more aggressive and I just kept pushing the boundaries."

As he became more assertive, it carried over into sports, which led to altercations on the basketball court too.

"To be honest, I was an angry kid," Chris said. "I started looking for fights all the time, but the more confident and aggressive I became, the more people started leaving me alone."

Chris's childhood provided many reasons to fuel his anger. His mother was only 15 years old when he was born. His sister was born two years later, and his father died a year later when he crashed his motorcycle over a cliff.

"My first childhood memory is flying to Las Vegas to live with my mom and her parents," Chris said. "We bounced around between her parents and a bunch of other places. I didn't even know who these people were. I just remember living in this ghetto apartment with parties and strangers around the house."

Those early years were chaos as his mother struggled to raise two children while she was still a child herself.

"They were always partying while my sister and I were running around the apartment," Chris said. "One day some dude unscrewed the leg of a chair and beat the shit out of another guy in the apartment."

Eventually things got so bad that Chris and his sister were put up for adoption until his grandfather picked them up and raised them in the Santa Cruz mountains.

"My grandfather was an old-school guy," Chris said. "If I was home I had to work. He had five acres with a cow, pigs, chickens and rabbits, so every morning I had to take care of all the animals. I hated the winter break because we had two weeks off from school and I spent the whole break pruning apple trees."

Chris's grandfather was a heavy equipment operator who grew up during the Great Depression. During construction projects, his grandfather brought scrap construction materials home for Chris to salvage the materials.

"I had to pull the nails out and use a hammer on an anvil to straighten and sort them by size," Chris said. "My grandfather wasn't poor, he just wouldn't throw anything away in case someone needed it someday."

Chris worked weekends and evenings during the winter, but during the summers, Chris had to put in a half-day's work before he was free for the afternoon.

"One year I dug a 150-foot-long trench by myself," Chris said. "I was out there alone every day digging in this 8-foot-deep trench with no one around, violating every safety rule. I hated it at the time, but I appreciated it when I got older."

Chris was hired for his first construction job in high school for $5 an hour. A week later the boss gave him a $1 per hour raise because he said Chris worked too hard.

"I didn't realize it at the time, but my grandfather taught me how to work," Chris said. "When I joined the workforce, I noticed that most people just don't know how to work."

Chris is grateful for the lessons, but it was not easy living with his grandfather.

"When I was young I was always trying to please my grandfather," Chris said. "He was an alcoholic who would become irrational and he wasn't the huggy type. I never heard, 'I love you,' nothing like that at all."

When Chris made typical childhood mistakes, his grandfather's discipline would certainly be considered child abuse by today's standards, but it was not all that uncommon for that generation.

"I got in trouble if I didn't anticipate what needed to be done next," Chris said. "I remember running in circles and he was whipping the shit out of me with a stick from my knees up to my back."

Chris did not have a father, and his mother was incapable of raising kids. He had already bounced around from home to home, so he felt like he had to walk on eggshells around his grandfather.

"I was always trying to please my grandfather because I felt like I needed his reassurance," Chris said. "I never knew what was going to happen, because he'd say some stupid shit sometimes."

One night, his grandfather came home late and Chris went to the car to help his grandfather walk in the house.

"He was hammered," Chris said. "I told him to come inside as I held the door open."

"Who the fuck are you to invite me in my own home," his grandfather snapped at him. "You don't have to live with us. We can send you somewhere else."

Chris knew his grandfather cared about him, but Chris lived in a state of anxiety worrying that he and his sister could be thrown out at any moment with nowhere to go.

Chris was friends with a few older boys whom he grew up with and admired.

"I started stepping out of my shell," Chris said. "I was drinking and partying a little with these guys on the weekends, and at first, it wasn't a big deal."

Anytime Chris wanted alcohol, his grandfather always had two refrigerators full of cans of Black Label beer.

"Every time I hung out with these guys, we started drinking," Chris said. "I got less reserved and started doing a lot of dumb things."

Chris had watched his grandfather's example for years. Every time they drove home from Santa Cruz, his grandfather stopped at the same liquor store to buy a 12-pack for the long drive home.

"Drinking and driving didn't seem like a big deal to me," Chris said. "I was a stupid kid, I just didn't perceive it as a threat."

During the summer when Chris was 16 years old, he went fishing at a pond with his friend, whose father worked with Chris's grandfather. They had been close friends ever since the first grade.

"We did a lot of stupid shit together all the time," Chris said. "We were both drunk that day and when I drove home, I hit a telephone pole at 70 miles per hour. I don't even know what happened, but it hit on the passenger side and tore the gray Toyota Corolla in half."

They were in the middle of nowhere, alone on a rural, two-lane road and Chris was unconscious.

"I woke up and no one was around," Chris said. "I took one look at my friend and he was lying next to me dead. I started freaking out."

A motorist called paramedics and they tried to calm Chris down, but he was hysterical.

"That was my best friend," Chris said in shock. "He's fucking dead."

They strapped Chris into an ambulance and took him to the hospital.

"I don't know how I lived," Chris said. "I was bruised up, broke a tooth, and had a bunch of glass in my face, but other than that, I was fine."

Chris's grandparents came to the hospital. They were supportive, but they were in shock that Chris's childhood friend was dead.

"From now on, whatever you do in your life, you have to do it for two people," his grandfather told him.

Once Chris was cleared from the hospital, he was booked into juvenile hall and spent the rest of the summer locked up until he was released to go to school and participate in sports.

"I don't think they would ever do that today," Chris said. "They were much more lenient back then, and by all appearances, I was a good kid. I got good grades. I was playing basketball and kind of doing all the things you're supposed to do, but every Friday night after my game, my grandfather drove me back to juvie. That was a huge motivation for me to start wrestling, because if I wasn't in sports, I was back in jail or working on the ranch."

When Chris was released from the hall, his sister introduced him to the high school wrestling coach.

"I fell in love with wrestling," Chris said. "I started devoting all my time to it. It wasn't verbalized, but I kind of figured out that if I kept myself out of the house, I wouldn't have to work."

Chris competed in the high school and freestyle wrestling season and played football too. On weekdays, he traveled to different schools to attend practices and then he competed in tournaments on the weekends.

On a typical day, Chris was on the bus by 7:00 in the morning for the one-hour trip to school. After school, he'd take a 30-minute bus ride to a different school for wrestling practice. At 8:30 in the evening he wrapped up the day after a 1½-hour bus ride home.

Every wrestling tournament and football game added time to Chris's sentence, but he eventually completed his time and never returned to the criminal justice system.

"There was a lot of shit going on in jail," Chris said. "Just seeing all that kind of straightened me up. I didn't want to deal with it, so I didn't drink for a long time."

When Chris completed his sentence, his grandfather took him to meet with his friend's parents.

"I had to face his whole family," Chris said. "That was one of the hardest things to deal with."

Chris was forced to attend counseling, but like most adolescents, he did not want to participate.

"I was very angry," Chris said. "I blamed myself for killing my best friend. I was only sixteen and I wasn't ready to grow up. I was pissed off at the whole situation."

Chris began to shut down.

"I mostly kept to myself," Chris said. "I wouldn't even say hi to people when they tried to talk to me at school."

Everyone who grew up in the rural area owned hunting rifles and that caused some concern for the people close to Chris.

"They took all my guns away," Chris said. "I don't think I

made comments, but they worried about suicide and it was probably warranted."

Chris used wrestling as a place to channel his anger.

"I'm not even sure how I got through it all," Chris said. "When I was wrestling, I would go as hard as I could. It just felt good to go super hard—almost out of control at times. I was always on the edge of being way too physical ... I don't know if it was anger ... maybe it was just being super competitive. I don't know."

Chris was not satisfied with winning wrestling matches.

"Even when I won, I was still unhappy," Chris said. "I didn't like to win by a little. When I was competing, I wanted total dominance. I wanted it to be perfect."

When Chris was fighting at his best, he lost awareness of what was occurring in the match.

"I don't even know what happens," Chris said. "I have to go back and deconstruct the fight to figure out what happened, but when it's going right, I can hardly recall a single thing."

Chris's coach saw something in him, so after high school, his coach helped him get in to Brigham Young University in Utah. At the time, it was one of the top 25 wrestling programs in the nation and a huge jump from the level of wrestlers he had been training with.

"I walked on the wrestling team and it was an awesome experience," Chris said. "I got pretty good, pretty fast, but I didn't realize it because I was surrounded by all these monsters."

Twice a year the 12 guys in his weight class cut weight and wrestled each other to determine the top wrestler on the team.

"I got up to fourth or fifth," Chris said. "I showed up and would get my ass kicked, but I felt pretty good about myself."

Chris did not have a scholarship like the other kids on the team. He was paying his own way through college, so he had to change his plans when the bill came in for his second year.

"I can't fucking do this," Chris said after seeing the exorbitant private school tuition bill. "When the school year ended, I moved back to California and went back to work."

Chris returned to his high school construction job. He was doing concrete, framing, and digging ditches, but it wasn't long before he was back to wrestling.

"A week before wrestling season started, I got a call," Chris said. "They asked if I wanted to be the high school wrestling coach. I said, 'Not really.'"

They did not have anyone else to fill the position, so Chris felt obligated to take it.

"Head coach at 20 years old?" Chris said. "I didn't want that kind responsibility. It caused me a lot of anxiety because I was in charge of all these kids and I was not used to it. I didn't have the tools at the time to deal with a lot of stuff that came up with teenagers."

Chris stumbled through the first year and ended up coaching for five years until he moved away to finish college. While he was coaching, he took community college classes, trying to figure out what he wanted to do with his career. When he read the description of an engineering class, he went in and met with the instructor.

"He had me in 10 minutes," Chris said. "He talked about weights, forces, and stuff. It was like solving a puzzle and I decided to be an engineer on the spot."

Chris was accepted into Cal Poly San Luis Obispo's engineering program, so he packed up his pregnant girlfriend and they moved. During breaks from school, Chris returned to Santa Cruz to pick up construction jobs to pay his way through school. During one of these visits, Chris discovered that Claudio Franca had opened a Jiu-Jitsu school in Santa Cruz. Chris had already attended the Rickson Gracie seminar and wanted to learn more.

"I wasn't really hooked yet," Chris said. "It was just another part of my grappling career. I had done American style and freestyle wrestling. I also did some Greco-Roman and a little bit of Judo along the way. To me it was just another grappling thing."

Claudio's school was new, so it was full of white belts.

"He would teach us a couple of moves and then we'd beat the shit out of each other," Chris said. "It was brutal. I got stitches and came home bloody all the time."

Because Chris only went to Claudio's academy during school breaks, he also joined a Judo club in San Luis Obispo and he earned his Judo black belt relatively fast.

"When I was a brown belt, I started beating some black belts in Judo competition," Chris said. "Judo is just another grappling sport, but with different rules. I got away with doing stuff from wrestling that you can't do now, like doubles and singles."

When Chris finished his engineering degree, he took a job in Santa Barbara where he met Richardo "Franjinha" Miller, the founder of Paragon Brazilian Jiu-Jitsu.

"Franjinha ran it like a wrestling class," Chris said. "It was an intense class and he would actually roll with us."

Chris was a blue belt in Jiu-Jitsu and had never rolled with a black belt before that first class at Paragon.

"I was a little apprehensive," Chris said. "I didn't know what the boundaries were."

Franjinha stopped in the middle of their sparring session and snapped at Chris.

"Don't look at the fucking belt," Franjinha said with his heavy Brazilian accent when Chris was holding back. "You just roll."

Chris was hooked on Jiu-Jitsu and for several years he drove between Santa Cruz and Santa Barbara to train and compete as he worked his way through the belts. He won the Pan Am and World tournaments as a purple belt.

By the time Chris received his brown belt, commuting long distances to academies was taking its toll. The group of people carpooling grew so much that they needed two cars to make the long drive.

"We had ten people carpooling and I realized that if we had our own place, it would save an hour and a half drive three times a week," Chris said. "But I wanted to be a student. I didn't want the responsibility of running a gym."

Chris was reluctant to become a teacher, just like he was reluctant to become a wrestling coach, but Franjinha was supportive and helped Chris open a Paragon Jiu-Jitsu academy in San Luis Obispo.

"It grew really slowly," Chris said. "I was still working full time, which is how I paid the $1500 rent for a year and a half before the gym started to break even."

Chris worked full time as an engineer and taught Jiu-Jitsu for free at night. It was working until he was promoted into management at the engineering firm.

"I was doing too much and getting burnt out," Chris said. "I was working 100 hours per week trying to juggle the business and work. Every time the phone rang, it was some emergency and I'd have to drop everything."

The economy took a downturn and his company began downsizing. There was a chance he could be laid off or relocated. Chris looked at the economics of his Jiu-Jitsu academy and realized that one gym would not financially sustain him if he left his job.

"I needed two gyms, two populations, to make it possible to live on," Chris said. "I talked to my wife about opening another gym, but she was against it. We had three kids and she needed the security of a steady paycheck. We started seeing things differently and it became one of the causes of our divorce."

Chris opened a second academy in a neighboring town and decided to leave his job.

"I agonized over it for about a week," Chris said. "It was scary. I had worked my way up to middle management and would be stepping away from a lot of money and a guaranteed paycheck. But I did the math and I figured I could live off almost nothing and just squeak by."

Once Chris made the decision, he felt a huge relief.

"I had all this stuff I was trying to juggle; engineering, family, business, and I was going through a divorce," Chris said. "When I focused on the Jiu-Jitsu business, it was just like being in class. I could just get wrapped up in it and all the other stuff would just go away. People love Jiu-Jitsu because it's an escape. When you go to class, you're forced to be in the moment. You can't be thinking about all this other shit that's happening in the other parts of your life."

When Chris focused on his business, he began to really enjoy being a teacher.

"In the early days, I was apprehensive about teaching," Chris said. "I didn't want to be responsible for someone else's Jiu-Jitsu, but then I began to see how it impacts so many people in a positive way."

After training for a year, one of Chris's students approached him after class.

"I want to thank you, coach. You saved my life," the student told Chris. "Without Jiu-Jitsu, I was angry and getting into fights. I was going through a divorce and sitting at home drinking all day. I'd be dead right now if it wasn't for Jiu-Jitsu."

His student's transformation was similar to what wrestling and Jiu-Jitsu had provided for Chris.

"I haven't gotten into a fight since I've started Jiu-Jitsu," Chris said. "I learned that it's really not worth it. I just see a lot of people upset and things get blown out of proportion, but there's nothing going on right now that can't wait until tomorrow when I'm not emotional about it."

All these years of training have changed his perspective.

"In my wrestling days, I used to look at my opponent like they were the fucking enemy," Chris said. "Today, I'm not angry anymore. These guys are cool, and I don't hold anything against them. When I'm rolling, it's not me against them. It's just me against the position."

Changing his perspective has allowed Chris to enjoy training in a different way.

"Even early on in my Jiu-Jitsu career, when I was training, I thought either I'm going to beat you up or you're going to beat me up. I've grown away from that. I can't go hard every day of the week. It just doesn't work for my body, or my mind. It doesn't do anybody any good. It doesn't grow the sport or the martial arts, but I still see people doing it today."

Today, Chris enjoys growing as an instructor as he constantly seeks better ways to help his students learn. His first formal instruction on teaching came when he took a three-week instructor course to teach at the police academy.

"I was taught how to teach," Chris said. "I started appreciating the art of teaching, so now I'm always trying to make myself a better instructor. I'm always trying to tweak it for different people because the four-year-old needs it said differently than a 30-year-old engineer. I appreciate smaller circles—all the little intricacies are so exciting because I'm seeing that there's so much more to learn."

By all appearances, Chris was a doing well as an engineer, making a great living, and climbing the ladder in his career.

"By many people's definition, I was successful, but I used to dread Sundays because I'd have to go to work on Monday," Chris said. "I'm very thankful that I found Jiu-Jitsu, because today, Sunday is great.

Monday I still work hard, make enough money to get by, but now I get to impact so many people's lives and have fun doing it."

Evandro Nunes

Evandro Nunes is a trainer at the world-famous Gracie Jiu-Jitsu University and has earned several world championship Brazilian Jiu-Jitsu medals.

His mindset toward fighting began forming while being raised by a tough Brazilian father who instilled strong, traditional values in him.

"If you see injustice toward you, or someone else, you stand up for it," Evandro's father taught him. "If you're wrong, you apologize, but if you're right, you fight for it."

Evandro was born with a firm sense of right and wrong, but it was his father's lessons that reinforced those instincts.

"It only made sense. If I'm right, I should win," Evandro said. "The good guy wins and the bad guy loses, just like in the movies."

That instinct led him into a lot of fights as a kid, many of which were with his brother, who was four years older.

"My brother and I fought a lot," Evandro said, "but I still remember the first time I won."

In this fight, Evandro was only seven years old and thought he could not possibly defeat his much-larger sibling.

"He punched me in the shoulder, and I fell on the floor crying," Evandro said.

Evandro's brother pushed him down four more times and then demanded that he stay on the ground.

"I remember feeling that I was right, so I should not lose," Evandro said. "I was willing to go as far as it took to defend my ground."

So Evandro stood up for the fifth time.

"My brother saw the look of determination in my eyes," Evandro said, "so he stopped and walked away. Physically I lost the fight, but mentally I won because I stood my ground."

Evandro got into his first street fight in the first grade. A bully was harassing his friends while they played a card game. When Evandro asked the bully to stop, the kid became aggressive.

"I didn't know Jiu-Jitsu, but I instinctively took him to the floor and got his back," Evandro said. "He was fighting, but I had both hooks in with the seatbelt grip."

Evandro's father encouraged self-defense, but he also taught him not to abuse his power.

"I did not want to hurt this guy," Evandro said. "I just wanted him to stop."

The kid promised to leave Evandro and his friends alone, so Evandro let him go.

"Then the bully stood up and punched me in the face," Evandro said. "It was my first black eye."

Evandro fell down and started crying in front of his friends. Then he ran to his brother and begged him to retaliate.

"I'm not fighting your fight," Evandro's brother calmly told him.

"It didn't make sense in my brain," Evandro said. "I was shamed in front of everyone. We were brothers, and he was supposed to defend me."

Evandro resented his brother for leaving him to deal with the bully on his own, but years later he realized how much his brother had actually forced him to grow.

"I lost the micro fight, but I won the macro fight." Evandro said. "It's better to have one black eye in the first grade than to be bullied for the rest of your life."

Had Evandro bowed to that bully when he was young, it would have ingrained the habit of not standing up for what he believed in.

"There was no more bullying coming in my direction," Evandro said. "That black eye prevented a lifetime of bullying. You become a victim when you bow to something you don't believe in. I'd rather be punched in the face once than be punched in my mind forever. That's much more abusive."

Evandro mentioned the power of our mind and the difficulty of recovering from mental abuse.

"What we tell ourselves matters," Evandro said. "I will become what my mind believes."

Evandro's parents divorced when he was 14 years old. During their family breakup, Evandro's parents disclosed for the first time that his father had adopted him.

"It was like a punch to my throat," Evandro said. "It was mind-blowing. The man who had been teaching me integrity my whole life had been lying to me for 14 years."

Evandro continued to have a healthy and loving relationship with his father, but that life-changing moment caused Evandro to begin questioning everything.

"I was oblivious to the idea that someone could lie to me," Evandro said. "I couldn't see it. Once that happened, I began my pursuit of the truth. I cannot live where I am not being honest."

Evandro did not realize it at the time, but it was discovering Jiu-Jitsu that later allowed him to live with complete integrity.

About the same time that his parents got divorced, he had a run-in with another kid.

"I wasn't the kind of person who was looking for trouble," Evandro said. "I was always defending myself or other people."

Evandro was walking down a street in Brazil when he was challenged by a big kid in the neighborhood. The argument began over a petty dispute about trading cards.

"He stole the cards from me, but he clearly needed them more than I did," Evandro said. "I was going to let him have those cards."

Someone asked Evandro if he wanted to fight the big kid. Evandro laughed and turned to walk away.

Then the big kid asked him if he was afraid.

Evandro stopped and looked back. He told the other boys he wasn't afraid.

Then he turned around and walked back to the big kid who was challenging him.

"I wasn't afraid," Evandro said. "Or maybe I was, I don't know."

But Evandro knew that if he had walked away, everyone would have believed he was afraid.

"I had to prove to him that I wasn't afraid," Evandro said. "Maybe I needed to prove it to myself. I lacked the confidence that I wasn't really afraid. I needed to prove it to everyone: him, my friends, and myself."

Evandro stood in front of the big kid and they stared each other down.

"I remember looking into his eyes," Evandro said. "I didn't even think he was going to fight. I thought we were going to exchange some words and walk away, but suddenly he head-butted me on my nose."

Evandro fell back and stumbled to the ground with a broken nose.

"I stood and stepped back," Evandro said. "I took two steps and 'boom!' I landed a full-power fist on his jaw."

The big kid got angry, shook his head, and started walking toward Evandro.

"That was everything I had," Evandro said. "I had just given him everything, with the bonus of a little run, but he just shook it off and kept walking toward me."

Evandro started retreating backwards.

"I was afraid I was going to die," Evandro said. "Because if that didn't work, I was done. I had nothing else."

Evandro ran and kept a safe distance, exchanging words, and choosing not to engage until he walked away.

"I remember thinking that I was defending myself," Evandro said. "The guy had taken my cards but for some reason he still wanted to fight. I could not see where I was wrong, but still I lost that fight."

That incident inspired Evandro to seek a better way to fight. Evandro was not sure where to turn, but he ended up in a weight-lifting gym with a friend, intending to bulk up with more muscle.

During their first visit to the gym, while Evandro's friend was in the restroom, Evandro watched vale tudo fighters hitting bags and rolling on the floor of the gym. While Evandro watched, the man who would become his first instructor, Mateus Detail, approached him.

"He was a law enforcement officer in Brazil," Evandro said. "He was like Guile from Street Fighter. A big, strong guy with a scar on his face."

The man was friendly and invited Evandro to join their workout.

"My friend came out of the restroom all excited to work out,"

Evandro said. "But I told him I wasn't lifting weights because I was going to try the vale tudo class."

That was Evandro's first day of training and, with time, he gravitated to the ground-fighting classes. After about a month of training, Evandro was partnered up with a fighter who he admired.

"I wanted to be like him," Evandro said. "He had a perfect physique and was the best guy at the academy back then."

That day in class, they learned the arm triangle choke from the side mount.

"There were only three details: frame, push, jump," Evandro said. "We drilled it five times each side and then we sparred."

When they started rolling, his training partner framed his neck just as they had drilled.

"I wasn't thinking about him," Evandro said. "I just did what I was supposed to do: step one, two, and three, and then I started holding. Suddenly, the guy started jumping like a fish out of water. I didn't even know what was happening."

Evandro realized the technique was actually working and his partner was in trouble.

"I kept holding it and then he tapped!" Evandro said. "That moment completely changed my life. I was this weak, skinny, 14-year-old kid. I had never tapped anyone, and suddenly I was tapping out the guy I looked up to."

After that class, Evandro went home and searched for Jiu-Jitsu online and discovered the old Gracie Challenge fights and the UFC. Those videos inspired him to seek out a gym that trained in the gi. He found an academy and trained there briefly.

"I rolled with an aggressive black belt," Evandro said. "He did leg and arm locks and popped all my joints. I didn't know what was happening, and he was hurting me. I trained there for a little bit, but it was not sustainable, so I found a new place."

On the first day at the new academy, the instructor, Marcio Barao, invited Evandro to participate in a tournament.

"Why are you asking me to compete?" Evandro asked his new instructor. "I don't even know anything."

The instructor encouraged competition and suggested that he just go for fun. That weekend, Evandro found himself at his first tournament. He was 15 years old and a new white belt.

"I was afraid, but I was curious," Evandro said. "I looked around, and I couldn't find any kids my age."

Evandro's instructor had registered him in the adult division.

"It was kind of normal for me to fight grown-ups," Evandro said. "I fought adults in the academies, and my brother was always much older. My whole life I never fought anyone my age. They were always bigger."

Before Evandro's first match, he watched other fights and saw the referees raise their hands and point cards being turned. Evandro asked about the rules and points.

"The rules are you don't get tapped and you tap them out," Evandro's coach said. "Just like we do in training."

Evandro never second-guessed that advice and adopted that as his own philosophy. In his first competition, he defeated every one of his opponents by submission.

That lesson from his instructor stuck with him his entire career. Evandro has never played the Jiu-Jitsu point game and instead always hunted for the submission.

"Control is a submission, it's just harder," Evandro said. "If you want to finish a fight in 30 seconds, you're not doing Jiu-Jitsu. But if I can control you for 10 minutes, and you cannot get up, it's like being locked in a box. How terrifying is that?"

Evandro continued competing regularly from white to brown belt.

"We fought every weekend that there was a competition," Evandro said. "Back then my friends were drinking and partying while I was traveling to tournaments three weekends out of the month."

Evandro explained that it was that persistence that led to his future success.

"I lost a bunch," Evandro said. "I was willing to lose all those tournaments, and that's why I'm here today. Many people lose one or two times and stop competing. But I say, 'Let's lose again and again.' And then eventually you become good.'"

When Evandro earned his brown belt, he was paying attention to Roger Gracie.

"I wanted to fight like this guy," Evandro said. "He doesn't even smile, nor does he celebrate too much. He takes them down, passes the guard, mounts, and finishes with a cross choke. He is a solid human being who is a very efficient example of Jiu-Jitsu."

At that time, many of Evandro's friends worshiped the Jiu-Jitsu stars of the time.

"I was not worshiping people, I was studying them," Evandro said. "I know that if another man can do it, I can too. If they're that amazing, I can be too."

There were things that Evandro did not admire about some of the top champions at the time. Evandro described matches where a fighter would squeak out a single advantage point and then use strength to stall. There were fights where the winner would be ahead by one advantage point, while in danger of a nasty arm bar, but the clock would run out.

"He almost lost," Evandro said. "Then time runs out, and he's a multiple-time world champion with no submission ever. He was about to lose, but these guys are freaking out, doing back flips, pulling open their gi and screaming to celebrate. That's crazy."

After Evandro watched these guys fight at the higher-level tournaments, he decided it was his turn.

"It was time to stop talking," Evandro said. "I thought I was better than those guys, and there was only one way to know. I needed to go there and fight them. My motivation back then was to prove to myself that I was better, and it was easier than I thought."

Evandro entered the IBJJF tournament in Brazil, which at that time was where the top fighters were competing. Evandro stayed true to what he learned at his very first tournament.

"I was not going to do points," Evandro said. "I went out there to choke people out, because that's the only thing I knew how to do."

Evandro won every match by submission, except the last.

"I had lots of nerves," Evandro said. "Back then I didn't understand energy efficiency. I was just brawling. I won three fights by submission and lost the fourth by points, so I didn't lose, time just ran out. At least that's how I see it."

Evandro continued competing regularly, but at that time, Metamoris was his ultimate goal.

"I knew that my skills were top-notch," Evandro said. "What I wanted to know was if I belonged in the top level of the Jiu-Jitsu community, and Metamoris would be my proof of that. There would be nothing else left for me to fight."

The evening before Metamoris 6, friends invited Evandro to watch the fight, but he had to decline because he was competing in Las Vegas.

"The way Metamoris happened is a beautiful story," Evandro said. "I told my friend that night that I had no idea when, but I knew I would eventually fight in Metamoris."

Josh Barnett was scheduled to fight Cyborg, but rumor spread that Cyborg was injured, so Evandro found the fight promoter's number and sent him a text message. They had never met, but Evandro felt he had nothing to lose.

"I was willing to fight Josh Barnett," Evandro said. "Who cares if you guys don't know who I am? I'm going to choke him out. That was my mindset until you prove me wrong."

Evandro sent the fight promoter a message mentioning his weight and titles, but he discovered that Ryron Gracie was already filling in for Cyborg.

The next day, Evandro flew to Las Vegas to fight in another event. While Evandro was warming up for his fight in Las Vegas, at the last minute, Jeff Moson backed out of the Metamoris event.

"The fight promoter called me seven minutes before my Vegas fight," Evandro said. "With two hours' notice he bought me a plane ticket, and I flew back to L.A. and fought in Metamoris."

The fight ended in a draw, and Evandro reached his goal of fighting in the live televised event, but what turned out to be more significant was his chance meeting with Ryron Gracie in the warm-up area.

"We connected not only with Jiu-Jitsu but also on a personal level," Evandro said. "Two months later I was teaching at the Gracie Academy."

Evandro's success and growth in Jiu-Jitsu also helped him grow as a person. Evandro attended a personal development seminar where he discovered unconscious resentment he had been holding on to his entire life. One of the seminar assignments was to write a letter to a family member.

"I started writing the letter to my brother, but I couldn't finish it." Evandro said. "My biggest realization was that I used to blame my brother for fighting with me too much and not standing up for me."

The seminar speaker had said that we like to blame people for what they did to us, but we don't like to give them credit for what they did for us.

"I called my brother and told him everything," Evandro said. "Suddenly I started crying when it became obvious that he was the best brother ever."

Like most brothers, they were competitive with each other, but in the early years, with the four-year age gap, Evandro could never keep up. Being the older sibling, instead of hanging out with Evandro, his brother preferred to hang out with older kids when playing soccer and video games, and doing everything else that young boys do.

"Because he didn't stand up for me in my first fight, I had to learn how to overcome my own battles," Evandro said. "Because he fought with me, I had to learn how to stand up for myself regardless of the consequences. Once I discovered that, I realized my brother was the best brother ever."

Much of Evandro's drive and ambition can be attributed to his desire to impress his older brother.

"I wanted his love and approval," Evandro said. "I felt loved and seen, but I didn't feel seen in the way I wanted to be seen. I figured that one day when I was faster in soccer, or better at video games, I'd be able to play with my brother."

Evandro pushed so hard to impress his brother that at some point he surpassed him.

"When I was 16 with a blue belt, he didn't want to fight me anymore," Evandro said. "Then I used to show him everything because I was trying to impress him. I'd say, 'Look at this, look at me, look at my gold medals.'"

In hindsight, Evandro realized that by trying so hard to impress his older brother, Evandro may have made his brother feel badly about his own achievements.

"As I was surpassing him, I made a point of showing him that I was better," Evandro said. "When I called him, I said I was sorry and said that he was the reason why I am where I am today."

At the end of their phone call, his brother cried, which was the first Evandro had ever heard him show that type of emotion.

Evandro attributes his own personal growth to Jiu-Jitsu, but the more important benefit of training was is that it gave him the courage to live honestly.

"My father is an honest man, but he is human with his own limitations," Evandro said. "I understand why he lied to me. He was coming from a place of fear. He was trying to protect me and himself, but seeing my dad not being able to live up to his words was a significant moment for me."

That event had such an impact that living honestly became Evandro's driving force in life. It was Jiu-Jitsu that became the tool that enabled him to live with integrity.

"Jiu-Jitsu gave me the confidence to be who I am," Evandro said. "Everyone wants to be who they really are, but they feel unable to because if everything goes wrong, they may have to fight. I think the ultimate fear of all humans is that they cannot physically defend themselves."

Evandro explained that being able to fight is not what is important.

"Having the confidence to be yourself is enough," Evandro said. "But learning how to fight is what gives you that confidence, and when you know how to fight, no one will want to fight you."

Evandro thinks that modern society has evolved in a way that we rarely need to fight anymore.

"In Brazil there were a lot of opportunities to be a hero," Evandro said. "Here in the United States, you rarely see people attacking someone in the street, so there are fewer opportunities to defend yourself, but the fear still exists inside people."

Evandro is less willing to get into a fight today than when he was a kid.

"Today, I don't see myself fighting unless there's a need to defend a life," Evandro said. "If a homeless guy spits on me, I can control myself. I'm the safest person to be spit on because I'm not reacting to things anymore."

Evandro's willingness to fight has deescalated as he has tried to understand where the other person is coming from. Evandro said he would feel the emotions of being spit on, but he would not take it personally.

"That person must be in pain," Evandro said. "Because I know I did nothing to deserve that. If someone cuts in front of me in traffic, I assume that person must really be in a hurry to do something that unsafe to gain four seconds. I can only imagine the mental prison this person is in."

Evandro explained that most fights between men stem from their insecurity about their ability to defend themselves.

"If two men bump into each other in the bar, they need to prove themselves to their wives, their friends, and themselves," Evandro said. "Insecurity is what caused the fight. I already know I can fight. I no longer need to prove myself because my self-worth is not based on someone else's perception. That's a byproduct of Jiu-Jitsu."

Learning self-defense skills are essential, but Evandro said that mindset is even more important.

"If I really believe in what I'm fighting for, I'm going to fight until I die," Evandro said. "I don't think most people are willing to go that far."

Evandro described, as an example, a drunken thug who starts a fight in the street.

"He knows he's causing trouble," Evandro said. "Somewhere in his subconscious, he knows he wants some attention. Therefore, he's not willing to die for that fight. Me, on the other hand, I'm walking in plenitude, peace, and love, so if someone starts a fight, I am only acting on what I truly believe in, and I'm willing to die for those things I truly believe in."

It took a lifetime of fighting for Evandro to find this sense of harmony.

"I feel in such a place of peace today," Evandro said. "There's nothing else I want in life. I don't need more money. I don't need outside approval. I don't need fame. I don't need anything external. I'm in such peace that I can live moment by moment."

Evandro said that historically, philosophers used to sit on top of a stone to think and write about life.

"A long time ago, a philosopher said, 'The only purpose in life is to give back as a form of performance whatever inspired you in the first place,'" Evandro explained. "Brazilian Jiu-Jitsu changed my life and has allowed me to pursue my dreams. So what I'm doing is repackaging what inspired me so I can perform as a teacher to share Jiu-Jitsu with my students in the most pleasant way possible. I'm giving back what inspired me."

Evandro's definition of success has not changed since he was a kid.

"Success is truly getting in touch with myself to know what I'm feeling and then being able to express it free of judgment or fear," Evandro said. "Success is being honest."

Garth Taylor

Garth Taylor was warming up, preparing for his fight at the Tijuca Clube in Rio de Janeiro. It was the day that brown and black belts were competing in the World Brazilian Jiu-Jitsu Championship. Garth noticed a commotion as paramedics fought their way through the crowd to get to one of the fighters.

"It was insane how many people were crammed into that venue," Garth said. "There was a guy who needed serious medical attention, but the medics couldn't even get to him because it was so crowded."

When medics reached the fighter, he was unresponsive.

"We were standing there about ready to fight as they worked that guy up and put him on a board," Garth said. "There was no exit down there, no way to get him out because the crowd was so big and nobody would move."

Another crew of medics stood on the second tier of the stadium, unable to get to the ground floor.

"They crowd-surfed him on a stretcher and took him out of the building," Garth said.

Garth stood there wondering what had happened but later learned the fighter died during his match from a heart attack. As Garth watched all of this unfold, he tried to focus on his fight for the world championship.

"I was on deck and started wondering what if that happens to me," Garth said. "I'm bigger than that guy. How in the hell are they gonna get me out of here? It was crazy."

*   *   *

Garth Taylor is a pioneer of Brazilian Jiu-Jitsu in the United States. He's won medals at every belt level in the World Jiu-Jitsu Championship in Brazil. Garth is a five-time US Open champion and a veteran of the invitation-only ADCC World Championship, and he has notable grappling wins over Ultimate Fighting Championship stars Ricco Rodriguez, Josh Barnett, and Gabriel Gonzaga.

Garth's Jiu-Jitsu career began when he joined the Santa Cruz High School wrestling team as a senior. The team had a thin roster, so he got a varsity spot his first year.

"I was wrestling guys who had been wrestling their whole lives, so I got my ass kicked," Garth said. "It was trial by fire. The learning curve was steep, but after a while, I started winning too. I think I ended my first year with 10 wins and 10 losses. Some of those losses were just ass whippings, but I did pretty good for coming in off the street."

Garth grew up in the Santa Cruz beach community, where everyone his age was a surfer.

"I think surfers are naturally good wrestlers," Garth said. "They've got balance, they're relatively strong, and they're used to doing stuff by themselves. When I went on to coach wrestling, I would always recruit surfer kids because I knew that they would be able to handle it. I mean, it's sink or swim in the ocean, right?"

Garth's brother and all his friends were professional surfers.

"I wasn't as good as them, but I loved surfing," Garth said. "It was hard to get anybody to go out for team sports in our town because everybody surfed, but when I finally went out for wrestling, I fell in love with it. It was the first time I prioritized something, and I got my life together. I'd grown up smoking pot, but that year, I quit and got focused."

Garth was attracted to wrestling for the same reason a lot of people avoid challenges.

"I loved how difficult it was," Garth said. "It was so friggin' hard—physically and mentally—and it's challenging to compete by yourself. I like being responsible for what happens: win or lose—you're on your own."

After high school, Garth continued his wrestling career in college.

"I had the same learning curve all over again," Garth said. "I was an inexperienced high school wrestler who was starting to figure it out; then I went to college as a very inexperienced wrestler trying compete at that level. It was tough, man. I got my ass handed to me all the time."

Garth had some wins his first year, but he lost his varsity spot before the state tournament.

"I lost it in a wrestle-off," Garth said. "There's only one spot, and there are 40 wrestlers in the room. You have to fight your way to the top of the room before you get to wrestle outside of the room. But I kept plugging away, and in my last year, I made it into the state tournament."

After finishing junior college, Garth returned to Santa Cruz High School, where he started coaching wrestling. That was when a friend told Garth, "You need to check out this street-fighting judo shit."

Not long after that, Garth watched the first UFC that was broadcast live on pay-per-view television.

"There's that street-fighting judo shit," Garth said, surprised as he watched Royce Gracie win the tournament. "It was the first time I saw a grappling martial art. My karate friends said wrestling was not legitimate, but as a wrestler, I knew different. Once I put my hands on you, I'm not coming off, but I didn't know submission holds. I knew these guys were doing forms and punching air, but every day in wrestling was combat. It's not even comparable."

About a month after the first UFC tournament, Garth saw a flyer advertising a Rickson Gracie seminar.

"I didn't know he was the greatest Jiu-Jitsu fighter of all time," Garth said. "I've been on the mat with very high-level wrestlers—national champions—but Rickson was different. I recognized it right away by the way he moved and carried himself. He was a masterful grappler."

Seminars are different today because everyone already knows that Jiu-Jitsu works. In the old days, Jiu-Jitsu seminars were about proving the effectiveness of Jiu-Jitsu. Rickson sat in the middle of a circle of 50 students, and one by one, he called out each student.

"I got to wrestle with him, and he immediately took my back and choked me out. It was so fast that I didn't even know what happened," Garth said. "He submitted one person after another. None of us knew Jiu-Jitsu, so it was probably easy pickings, but it was still 50 guys that he tapped in a row. He didn't dodge anyone, and there were some big, strong wrestlers in there."

Watching Rickson roll at that seminar hooked Garth, and he immediately started training in Jiu-Jitsu. He trained with a few instructors until he found Claudio Franca, with whom Garth trained for 12 years.

"I was Claudio's first black belt," Garth said. "I competed like a madman before I got my black belt. I fought everywhere I could.

32

Every year, I went to Brazil to fight in the world championships. Back then, there were only about five Americans competing in Brazil. I might be the first non-Brazilian to medal at every belt level at the World Jiu-Jitsu Championship."

UFC champion B.J. Penn and Garth were training partners in Santa Cruz when they were brown belts. That year, Penn went to Brazil expecting to compete as a brown belt, but he was unexpectedly promoted to black belt. In Penn's first black belt competition, Penn became the first non-Brazilian world champion.

Garth was an average wrestler, but he excelled in Jiu-Jitsu. Garth started wrestling late, so he was always behind his peers, but in Jiu-Jitsu, he was ahead of the curve.

"When I started Jiu-Jitsu as a white belt, I had a lot of wrestling and competition experience," Garth said. "Instead of wrestling uphill, I had an early advantage. That confidence made me feel like I was ahead of the curve, and that helped me become very successful."

Garth's success in Jiu-Jitsu caused him to love the sport even more.

"It was the first thing I was truly good at," Garth said, "and it was the first time I got recognition for something. Where I grew up in Santa Cruz, if you weren't a pro surfer, you were nothing. The town was loaded with really high-quality surfers, and that was how you earned status."

Winning in competition filled a void that Garth had lived with for much of his youth.

"Wins brought more of the things I wanted," Garth said. "I was trying to do something that mattered and would get me recognition. I was able to get more of the attention and acceptance I needed because my peers put me on a pedestal every time I won. That validated that I was relevant."

Growing up with an older brother was difficult because it was hard for Garth to measure up to someone who was older and more gifted.

"It's tough to live in someone's shadow," Garth said. "He was a professional surfer in a community where surfing was the number-one valued thing. Everybody loved him, and I never felt good enough."

Garth admires his brother's accomplishments in surfing and today as a carpenter and family man, but his desire to measure up to his brother drove Garth to eventually surpass his brother's athletic accomplishments. Winning in Jiu-Jitsu helped Garth cope with feelings of inadequacy, but losing brought him shame and embarrassment.

"I have some self-worth issues, so losses cause me to question if I'm really supposed to be there," Garth said. "Maybe I was lucky. Maybe all of it was a fluke. But it's not, because I've been smashing guys at every belt level. But those moments still come, because a loss takes me back to everything that happened to me as a child."

When Garth was four years old, his parents divorced, and his father slowly drifted out of his life. In Garth's teen years, he'd see his father only once a year.

"My dad decided it was too much trouble to be in my life. Now he's not in my life at all," Garth said. "I wasn't good enough to keep my dad around. That's how I took it."

Garth grew up in chaos without a father, and his mother, who is a wonderful person, struggled as an alcoholic.

"You grow up fast when you're the child of an alcoholic, because a lot of times you've got to do the parenting—you've got to pick up the pieces," Garth said.

Garth subconsciously used his success in Jiu-Jitsu competition to overcome his childhood pain. That continued until the final black belt match of the Jiu-Jitsu world championship in Rio de Janeiro.

"It was a big moment for me," Garth said. "I finally got to the finals, and there was a lot at stake. The crowd was going nuts like only a crowd in Brazil can. When you go to the world championships now, it's nothing like it was in Brazil. You've got to go there. You've got to see the passion. It's in their blood—the passion—it's crazy."

After the long wait, the black belt final match started. Garth won the takedown and ended up in Marcio Corleta's guard.

"Corleta went for a flower sweep," Garth said. "When I based out on the sweep, he hit a bump sweep and went to mount. I was mounted and down six to two, but I heard my coach yelling that there were only 30 seconds left.

"I think about that match all the time because I was losing focus. I was looking at the crowd during the match. I was not able to maintain focus and concentrate, and all of this was going on in my final match for the black belt world finals."

"Thirty seconds!" Garth's coach yelled again. "You've got to go."

"I just bridged," Garth said. "I shoved my arm out thinking he'd probably go after my arm and I'd be able to get out of there and make something happen. Then it happened. What the fuck was I doing? I just fucked this up. I remember a distinct feeling of shame and embarrassment that I had just let this happen and there was nothing I could do about it. Corleta finished the arm lock."

Garth hardly remembers his victories, but he remembers every moment of every defeat.

"The losses that eat at me and keep me from sleeping are the ones where I didn't respond to the pressure," Garth said. "If somebody beats me because they're a lot better, I'm fine with that. I will go back to the gym and work on it and come back better, but the losses where I let other things affect my performance are the ones that just hurt."

Garth took that loss hard until he returned home and realized that he had just won a silver medal in the world championship.

"I got over the feeling of shame of that loss when I started to appreciate what I'd accomplished," Garth said. "I was the first foreigner to take second place in the world as a black belt, but when I got home, none of my regular friends really cared. That's when I kind of changed. I realized that I was not going to get the affirmation I was chasing, and I didn't really need it. I started to feel satisfied with my achievements, and I became less interested in competition."

When Garth was younger, he did not understand the forces that unconsciously drove him. It was not until he was 44 years old that he took an emotional intelligence course in Las Vegas and he began to understand all these things.

"It was one of the best things I've ever done for myself," Garth said. "I started to figure out some of the limiting self-beliefs that stemmed from my dad, and that helped me to get past them. I started to understand why I was on the hamster wheel, dating the same girls over and over. The same girl, but with different names.

"The course taught me to take personal responsibility for everything that happens in my life instead of playing victim. No matter how unfair it seems, if you take responsibility for everything, you don't give your power away, which gives you the power to change it.

"It helped with my self-worth issues," Garth said. "I realized that my dad was just a person who was struggling like everybody else. My mom is an alcoholic, but she is doing the best she can. I was just a kid, and their choices were not my fault."

Garth is grateful that he had Jiu-Jitsu to help him get make these discoveries.

"Jiu-Jitsu gave me the platform to follow my dreams and feel validation," Garth said. "It gave me the chance to work through my issues of self-worth and express myself in a positive way instead of a negative pursuit. Many of the friends I grew up with got caught up with drinking or methamphetamine. Jiu-Jitsu kept me focused during a time in my life when it could have been very dark. It kept me on the straight and narrow and gave me a focus."

As Garth's desire to compete diminished, he focused more on coaching.

"I love teaching Jiu Jitsu," Garth said. "I really believe it changes people's lives. I see a guy when he first starts—he's not strong, he's not mobile, he's not flexible, and he's certainly not confident. You can watch people get stronger and fitter, they walk standing straighter, and they have more confidence in all areas of their life.

"They get into a community of people who are just like them," Garth said. "There's nothing like the friends you get in Jiu-Jitsu. The people you share that experience with are something special. It changes their confidence, it changes their capabilities, and it changes their lives. I get to watch when it creates a sense of community and ownership. I like to see them chase their dreams like I got to chase mine. I just love being a coach. It gets me fired up every day. I don't know how else to say it."

Jerome Roseborough

Jerome Roseborough is the owner of Katy Brazilian Jiu-Jitsu Revolution Team Academy in Texas, but he discovered Jiu-Jitsu when a friend invited him to train in a small room in an apartment complex.

"It was not even a class," Jerome said. "We did not have mats, so we just rolled on the carpet. We ended up smashing out a window, and I had rug burns all over my elbows. I loved it."

They trained together for a few months and eventually bought some mats and invited other friends. After training there for about a year, Jerome moved to Texas and immediately joined Katy BJJ as a white belt.

"Before that first day, I didn't realize there was Jiu-Jitsu in a gi," Jerome said. "Probably like everybody else who walks in, I wasn't grasping the concept of how the gi was working against me."

Jerome was amazed that smaller and weaker guys were crushing him.

"I've noticed there are two types of people who try Jiu-Jitsu,"

Jerome explained. "One person's ego is so fragile that they will never come back, but the other comes back determined to learn it."

Jerome has never had an inflated ego. In fact, he felt he was on the other end of the spectrum as the weaker or insecure person, so discovering Jiu-Jitsu gave him hope.

His attitude toward growth in life and Jiu-Jitsu developed during a tumultuous journey that began when he was homeless and living in a car as a child.

Jerome's father wasn't around when he was born, and his mother raised five kids alone by working in a department store. Jerome's mother was fired after she was injured at work, and she was denied workers' compensation payments. When the money dried up, they were evicted from their home and the family was split up. Jerome's sisters were sent to a foster home, and his mother and second-oldest brother moved into a friend's house.

"Everything was going all right," Jerome said, "but then it all seemed to fall apart when she got hurt at work."

"I don't remember how it all happened, but my brother and I were living in a guy's cramped apartment," Jerome said. "We only stayed there for a little while because there was no room for us. That's when we started living in the car."

His mother did not know, but at 10 years old, Jerome and his 12-year-old brother moved into a small green Fiat car that was abandoned in the ghetto.

"I don't remember details of that time period," Jerome said, "but I clearly remember going to the grocery store every day to steal food to eat."

One day, a man from the neighborhood approached the car that had become Jerome's home. The man peered into the dirt-covered windows, trying to see if Jerome and his brother were sleeping in the car.

"We didn't say anything and tried to hide," Jerome said, recalling when the man called out their names.

Before long, Jerome and his brother were living in the man's small studio apartment that was attached to the alley.

"It's like a recurring nightmare," Jerome said. "It is always dark. I can't see the furniture, but I can feel and smell everything associated with it."

Jerome did not have a sense of how long they lived with the man, but Jerome waited 25 years before telling anyone what happened.

During those days, basketball became Jerome's way of coping with the pain of his childhood.

"If I was dealing with something, I went and played basketball," Jerome said. "Not to find the answer, but as a way to escape."

Jerome loved playing basketball, so he invested every spare minute of his days on the court and never left home without a basketball.

"I felt that's what separated me from the other players." Jerome said. "I was so sure of my skill set that I felt I could do anything in basketball, whereas, in other parts of my life, I didn't."

Jerome credits his high school junior varsity coach, Doug Peters, with having a significant impact on him.

"He was basically my Bobby Knight," Jerome said, referring to the coach who was famous for his fiery, aggressive coaching style. "If Coach Peters saw potential in you, he rode you. He wanted you to live up to your potential. Some don't perform well if there's a bunch of yelling in your face, but that's the type of coach I needed."

Jerome excelled on the court, but there were consequences of using the court to hide from the trauma of his childhood.

"Did he do something to you!?" the coach yelled at Jerome. "Because you just fouled the shit out of him."

Sometimes Jerome would respond emotionally and lash out in

anger. Other times he just shut down. Jerome's coach seemed to understand his family situation and took him under his wing.

"Coach Peters was not only teaching me basketball, but also how it parallels life," Jerome said. "As tough as he was on me, he seemed to understand my anger and the way it affected how I played."

"When you're out of high school you might have a boss like me," Coach Peters told Jerome. "You're going to have friends and family and they're going to disappoint you. They will be critical and do things you do not like, but you have to find a way to deal with it. You can't deal with the world like that. It can't happen."

"Sometimes I wondered why he was singling me out," Jerome said. "But in retrospect, he was right on the money, and it needed to be said. When I think about all the people in my life, I'm not sure any of them would have taken the time to do that."

Jerome explained that his anger stemmed from being afraid of losing, but he admitted that it was more complicated than that.

"I needed people to see me in a certain way," Jerome said as he paused to think. "I needed to play so people in the stands would think, *I want to be like him*. Spectators are not rooting for the supporter, they're rooting for a star."

Many of the times Jerome was emotional on the court, it was because he was terrified of letting his coach down.

"Coach Peters took the time while other people in my life were not paying attention to me," Jerome said. "I was conscious of that, and I wanted to make sure that after the game, he wouldn't have any critique of me."

Outside of the basketball court, Jerome moved through life in the shadows because he was afraid of people noticing him.

"Ever since I can remember, I've been kind of a loner. I'm pretty quiet, reserved, and shy, but when I played basketball I felt alive and that I could be me."

42

Jerome's drive to get on that pedestal in sports became more than a passing desire.

"If I was not the star, I'd be a failure," Jerome said. "It would prove all the lies that I used to tell myself."

When Jerome was 17 years old, for the first time that he knew of, his father reached out and wanted to meet him. Jerome was reluctant, but agreed.

"I grew up angry," Jerome said. "I was mad at my dad, and I certainly didn't feel like I mattered."

When his father arrived, he spent a little time alone with each of the kids. When it was Jerome's turn, they went for a walk around the block and his father started offering advice about life.

"Who the fuck are you?" Jerome thought as he quietly listened to his father for the first time in 17 years. *"You don't even know me and you think you're going to give me advice?"* That was the end of it. We didn't talk after that."

Jerome held onto that anger for over a decade. It wasn't until he heard a quote from Oprah Winfrey that he began reevaluating his perspective.

"Forgiveness is giving up the hope that the past could have been any different. It's accepting the past for what it was, and using this moment and this time to help yourself move forward."

Jerome thought about that quote for a long time as he struggled to understand how it applied to him. It was not until the terrorist attacks of September 11 that he began seeing a new perspective.

"I don't know why, but that changed everything," Jerome said. "I wanted to do some things differently."

For the first time, Jerome was open to reuniting with his father. It took several steps to get there, but eventually they sat down and were able to have an open conversation.

"My biggest problem is that I've never heard an apology from you," Jerome told his father. "I've never heard, 'I'm sorry.'"

"What do you want me to do?" Jerome's father answered. "I can't change the past."

"That used to kill me," Jerome explained. "I was going to lose it if he told me that one more time."

They continued to spend time together, but their relationship struggled until Jerome went on a trip with his father.

"There's still this underlying thing," Jerome's father said. "We're talking and spending time together, but it's like you're still mad."

"You're right," Jerome replied. "I don't think you get it! Why weren't you there? I was the little boy who wished he got a phone call and birthday cards from you. I wanted to know that you were thinking about me. That you cared. I had to seek that out in other people."

Jerome's father finally opened up about his own struggles of living on the streets and being involved with drugs. His father had even been shot once.

"When he finally told me his story, I felt so dumb," Jerome said. "I felt so bad that I had been feeling this way about him when he was battling his own demons. I never considered the fact that he hadn't abandoned me, it was that he didn't even have the capability to take care of me even if he wanted to. Because I was older, I was finally able to look at it from somebody else's perspective. It clicked for me that there was another side to this story."

That moment was the first time in Jerome's entire life that he had the answer to the question that had been controlling his whole life.

"Once he told me, I understood," Jerome said. "It was a bit of validation. It wasn't that my father didn't want to, but that he couldn't."

Jerome decided to give therapy a try. He was having some marriage issues, but there was more bubbling to the surface that he could not articulate. For the first time, Jerome opened up and told someone his personal story.

"I started to understand things I did not previously know," Jerome said. "Once I knew, I became accountable and I could no longer do nothing."

Jerome realized that he had made a choice to live as an angry person and that he was blaming his father for all the problems he had ever faced.

"I was addicted to that mindset," Jerome said. "It was like I wanted to be angry. I didn't want it to go away because it was fueling me. I didn't know what to replace it with. That's why I was reluctant to let it go. It had become my identity."

After speaking to his father, Jerome felt he had lost the ability to continue blaming his father. Jerome's father was responsible for his choices, but Jerome was finally able to apply Oprah's quote about forgiveness.

"I realized that if I could be open to that possibility that my life could have been the same even if he had been there, that allowed me to start uncovering other things I needed to change. I realized I was being affected by the past, and it had a strong hold on me."

Jerome believed that if his father had been present, none of the bad things would have happened to him.

"It came to a point where I had to look in the mirror and say, 'okay, I've outplayed this," Jerome said. "I felt like I held onto it as long as I could, but now I had to do something about it."

Jerome spent his entire life blaming his father for any of his short-comings, but now he was ready to take responsibility.

"That's when Brené Brown came into my life and turned it upside down," Jerome said. "A friend sent me a link to her vulnerability speech and I felt like she was talking directly to me."

Before Jerome had the conversation with his father, he blamed being abandoned for his troubles, but then he realized there were two separate issues that had been controlling him.

Through Brené Brown, Jerome came to understand that he was using his story of abandonment as an excuse to be angry, but in reality, he was using anger to avoid his deep fear of shame.

When he was 10 years old, homeless, and living in a car, the man that lured Jerome into his home had been molesting him. Jerome already felt that his father did not want him, and now this man was offering to take him in. Jerome feared that if he told anyone, he would be homeless again. Jerome was more willing to suffer in silence than risk having to sleep on the streets again.

"I knew that it was bad," Jerome said. "But I didn't look at it like he was bad. I internalized it and felt like I could never tell anyone. The shame of it was so great that saying anything would have been unbearable. I felt dirty and disposable, so my self-esteem and self-worth played out that way."

Jerome related closely to Brené Brown's teachings about shame and avoidant behavior.

"As a kid, I always walked looking down," Jerome said. "I felt that if I looked at people they would see me, they would see what happened. They would be able to see his fingerprints on me or the hue of his breath."

Prior to learning from Brown, Jerome had been mislabeling his feelings of shame. He quoted Brené Brown.

"Shame is a focus on self, guilt is a focus on behavior. Shame is 'I am bad.' Guilt is 'I did something bad.'"

"Once I was able to understand that, I realized that was exactly what I had been doing in all of my personal and professional relationships," Jerome said. "I was able to clearly see my pattern when shame was triggered."

Before Jerome was able to heal and share his story, he dove into every talk and book that Brown cited.

"I bought the book *Daring Greatly*, and it became my mantra," Jerome said. "Anything showing vulnerability, to me, was displaying absolute weakness. I did everything not to be viewed that way. I walked around with a scowl on my face so people would not think I was soft. I did everything I could to show that I would just wreck you if you bothered me."

To some degree, that defense mechanism worked for Jerome when he was young. It helped him survive by keeping people at arm's length and it fueled his drive in basketball; but once he got married and had kids, he did not have a way to shut it off.

"It started impacting my personal relationships," Jerome said. "It was 'my way or the highway.' I did not understand that I didn't need that anymore, so a lot of people paid along the way."

After these discoveries, Jerome realized that he was the common denominator in all of his problems. He decided that regardless what happened in the past, it was up to him to change.

"I decided I have to get a handle on this," Jerome said. "When I decided I have to do my work, that's when it just started changing."

Jerome called his ex-wife out of the blue. He explained what had been going on and then apologized.

"What's interesting is, 10 years earlier, I would have never done that," Jerome said. "I would never have been open to the idea because I was not self-aware enough to know there's value in being open to somebody else's influence. I was the loner, I needed to do it all. I needed to have total control. I think that's probably why my recovery was more delayed than it needed to be."

Jerome has overcome an overwhelming amount of adversity to get to where he is today, and he credits his mother's example as his model for perseverance.

"My mother raised five kids by herself," Jerome said. "She was injured at work and our dad wasn't there. She had all these things stacked against her. Nobody would've blamed her if she had said, 'You know what, this is too much. I can't do this anymore.' She could've used all of these excuses, but she didn't. She stuck it out, and she even went back to school."

When Jerome was growing up, he used to deal with a lot of racism.

Jerome's mother told him, "Every time somebody calls you a name, you can fight them or you can thicken your skin. At some point, you're not going to be able to fight the whole world."

"At first, that made me mad because it's not fair," Jerome said. "For a long time I thought, 'I guess I'll be fighting for a while.' But then it started to get tiring."

When Jerome looks back at those times, he realizes he was using those opportunities to fight as an excuse to blame his father. He wasn't fighting those particular people, he was fighting his father, just like he had dreamt many times before. But when he looks at the lessons he learned from his mother, he sees that she never made excuses.

"She was preparing us for how the world was really going to be," Jerome said. "Because the real world isn't going to care about our excuses. That's the way she raised us."

Jerome's journey of personal growth through adversity is what prepared him to take on his current role as instructor and owner at Katy BJJ. As Jerome worked his way through the belts in Jiu-Jitsu, his instructor was grooming him as a teacher, until he ultimately handed the reins over to Jerome.

Before Jerome's personal development, he was driven by anger and shame. Today he is driven by his passion to mentor his students in the same way that others were a mentor to him.

"My desire to get better is still there, but it's not what drives me anymore," Jerome said. "I want my students to succeed before I do as an individual competitor. I'll still compete, and I have aspirations in the sport, but that comes secondary. When I watch a student start on their first day, and watch the growth that happens, that's more rewarding than what I'll get out of competing."

Today, Jerome is able to use his platform as an instructor to guide other men through life just as his basketball coach did for him.

"When I hear someone talk about their struggles, I get to use Jiu-Jitsu as the opening to throw something out to see if they're in a place to receive it," Jerome said. "But they have to get to a certain point before they can even address it."

Jerome's model of the world has changed as he's grown and become more self-aware. Today, his measure of success has less to do with him and more to do with his students.

"Success would be one of my students owning their own studio." Jerome said. "To be able to groom somebody the same way my mentors did for me. That would be super awesome."

John Marine

John Marine and his friend filled a shopping cart full of booze, but as both were 16, neither was old enough to buy liquor.

"We grabbed the gallon jugs of Jack and vodka and ran for the car," John said. "He cracked a bottle of vodka. I opened the whiskey and we started pounding."

John had just broken up with his high school girlfriend, and his friend's girlfriend had just announced that she was pregnant.

"That first breakup was traumatic," John said. "It was devastating, because I had so many other issues from my childhood that I hadn't made good with. Losing my first girlfriend was just way too much."

The more they drank, the more they feed off each other's depression. After enough alcohol, they got ahold of a long rubber hose and then picked up a couple of friends for a road trip to Magic Mountain.

"We were out of our fucking minds when these guys hopped into the car with us," John said. "They could tell something was up, but they were a little nutty too, so everybody could have expected us to be a bit off."

Before picking up the last two guys, John and his friend had already agreed that after their night of partying at Magic Mountain, they were going to connect the hose to the exhaust and gas themselves.

"I was fucking serious," John said. "I didn't give a shit back then and I would've done anything."

The four of them made it about twenty miles before pulling off the highway when they reached a small town. There, a group of ten random guys provoked a fight with John's friends.

"Then a cop cruised up out of nowhere and had me sit on the curb," John said, "I told him my name was 'Mike Hunt.' It was the first fake name that popped in my head."

John Marine's father's last name was Martinez and his mother's is Gonzalez.

"I don't know where my real name came from either," John said. "I'm guessing my dad was involved in something illegal and had to change my name when I was young. That's my best guess from what I've gathered, because every time I asked, my grandparents told me not to worry about it."

The officer told John to stay on the curb as he walked back to the police car to run John's name through their system.

"The adrenaline made me feel sober, so I took off running," John said. "I was about to get away, until the alcohol caught up to me and I fell and hit my head on the ground."

John scrambled through a ditch trying to hide in a pile of leaves until the cops surrounded him with guns and a dog. John was arrested, but not booked into jail because he was a minor.

"It was a pivotal moment in my life," John said. "The cops had no idea, but I was down and out, and they saved my ass. I was 100 percent out of control and on the verge of suicide."

* * *

John had always been good at making friends, so he never got into fights, but he was still interested in martial arts.

"I was into Ninja Turtles and I loved Bruce Lee," John said. "I'd listen to them spew all that old-school martial arts wisdom about the journey of self-discovery, and I knew I needed that."

John did not have anyone who encouraged him to participate in sports or extracurricular activities, so he craved direction in his life.

"I was such a cluster fuck at that age, so I was looking for something," John said. "I was seeking out people who could show me what it was like to have a dad. I was looking for someone to take care of me like I was their kid."

John's neighbor introduced him to Isaiah Rivera, a trainer who was teaching fighters Vale Tudo, the term Brazilian fighters used for "anything goes." Vale Tudo has since morphed into what is known today as mixed martial arts.

"Isaiah was my first actual coach," John said. "He was somebody I looked up to at a time when I needed it. I was a little kid and Isaiah was larger than life—strong, confident, and charismatic. At times, he was a Neanderthal caveman—and at other times he was this polite, intellectual guy. He was the sensei, father figure, crazy older brother, and friend. He was everything I needed at the time, and I still thank him to this day."

John was seeking a male role model because he had been separated from his father before starting elementary school.

"I have these crazy memories from before I was four years old," John said. "My dad was a heroin addict and would take me with him to pick up dope down the street."

When John and his father got to the dope house, John had to wait outside while his father went in with a woman.

"They'd kiss at the door and then my dad would go to the back room with her," John said. "The only reason I remember him picking up dope and cheating on my mom is because he left me outside crying with a big ass German shepherd tied to a chain. It would run at me barking with his teeth snarling and everything. It was traumatic."

John said, with sarcasm, that he lived in a great part of town, because on the walk home, they stopped to watch a man standing on an apartment balcony surrounded by cops.

"The guy was waving a butcher knife in one hand and a whiskey bottle in the other," John said. "He was freaking out and screaming at the cops who were pointing their guns at him."

The man threw the knife and it stuck in the door of another apartment.

"Some old man opened the door after the knife stuck in it," John said. "He probably thought the police were knocking to interview him or something. The old man opened the door and I can still see his reaction when he saw the knife and then slammed the door shut."

After the man threw the knife, the police tackled him.

"The cops didn't shoot you back in the day," John said. "They'd Rodney King your ass first, which you were lucky to get if you were acting like a fucking idiot."

John is surprised he can remember these events with such clarity from such a young age.

"In retrospect, it's funny that I'm able to put this story together from what happened when I was four years old," John said. "But I'll never forget these moments for the rest of my life because these traumatic experiences are hardwired into my brain."

The final straw came when John's grandmother visited and found him virtually dead in his crib. At almost four years old, John was too old for a crib, but his parents threw him in there, so they would not have to deal with him.

"My dad had passed out with a needle in his arm," John said. "My grandmother freaked out and took me to the hospital. The doctor said I was almost dead because I had not eaten for three or four days. That's what happens when you're on a drug binge."

Child Protective Services intervened until John's grandmother stepped in to raise John and his sister. Soon John's mother also moved in with them because she was developmentally disabled from a complication at birth.

"I always had animosity toward my dad, but it's touchy with my mom," John said. "At ten years old, I remember being confused, wondering why I was in the position of telling my mom what was right and wrong. She called me the other day and said, 'John, Metallica is playing.' It's like your ten-year-old daughter is calling. It's cute, and I want go, 'Oh, okay sweetie. Thanks for calling.'"

John is incredibly grateful that his grandmother took him in, but the hardship of being between his mother and grandmother put him in a very painful position.

"I always treated my grandma like she was my mom," John said, "but she would push me away. She constantly denied that role, and I still deal with it."

John pleaded with his grandmother to accept the maternal role that he needed.

"This lady's not stepping up to the plate," John said about his mother. "My grandmother fed me, took care of me, and loved me more than anybody, but she would never admit responsibility."

As an adult, John has a better understanding of the situation.

"I think my grandmother wants me to develop a relationship with my mom, so she doesn't have to worry who will take care of her when my grandmother is gone," John said. "It's a dilemma for her, but it's just as much of a dilemma for me. I didn't ask for any of this, but I never got my needs met either."

While John was looking to his grandmother to fill the maternal role, he also hoped his grandfather would be able to fill the role of the father he never had.

"My grandfather wasn't much of a father figure," John said. "I looked up to him, but when I look back, I realize he didn't want any part of it. We never had a great connection, and he ended up leaving my grandma for a while."

Once John's grandfather left, John became increasingly rebellious, but when his grandfather returned, John became angry and resentful.

"I was pissed when he came back," John said. "We had this thing going on and I didn't want him to fuck it up for me. When he was gone, grandma let me do whatever I wanted, but men are strict. I was kind of puffing up my chest, and he was flexing his muscle too, but at the same time, he must have felt his place was a little bit compromised after leaving."

John was angry because of the betrayal he felt from not having the family support he needed, while at the same time, he was going through the challenges of adolescence.

"By the time I got to high school, my grandfather had returned, but nobody was telling me shit," John said. "I became this rebellious punk rocker and anything was possible."

John's grandmother was concerned, but she was distracted trying to rekindle the relationship with her husband and had lost control of John.

"I'd wake up in the morning before school and say, 'What's up, Grandma,' while I was pouring a flask of whiskey in front of her. I would jump on trains and travel out of town and just sleep in the back like a squatter. I was in a place where there was no stopping me."

When John started training Vale Tudo with Isaiah, it gave him a place to channel his anger, but after about a year, he put it aside to pursue his passion for music.

"I joined a band with some tight-knit guys," John said. "I played bass guitar, and I poured all my emotion, heartache, and everything into music."

John is a sensitive person, and music allows him to feel his emotions.

"I didn't have parents to go to when I needed it," John said. "Men are expected to shut out our emotions, shrug it off, and deal with it. The next best thing was hearing a song that would hit me at my core and allow me to feel what I needed to feel."

After John graduated from high school, he left home and went with his friends to attend the Musician's Institute in Hollywood, California.

"I learned a lot and it helped me understand music at another level," John said, "but the best part of it was probably also the most disappointing."

John discovered that the level of talent surrounding him in Hollywood was significantly different than he was used to in his small town.

"I thought I was awesome," John said. "But when you go to music school you learn how much you really don't know. I saw how much better other people were, and I started beating myself up a little bit. I was surrounded by talented musicians and actors. The girl who sat next to me in class played Pocahontas in *The New World*."

After years of training in Jiu-Jitsu, John has a very different perspective today.

"That was foolish thinking," John said. "Because it doesn't matter how amazing somebody is, we all have something to offer. What matters is that you're stylistically true to yourself."

John paraphrased one of the lessons he heard from Bruce Lee.

"Express yourself truly. Express yourself honestly. If you can do that, then everything you do is beautiful."

John played gigs at the famous Los Angeles bars during his years in music school.

"It was a really good experience," he said, "but L.A. can suck the life out of you, so I left."

When John returned to his hometown of Santa Maria, California, he worked at a winery while doing background acting jobs on TV shows. He was in shows like *The Unit* and *CSI, NY*.

While John was gone, a new Brazilian Jiu-Jitsu school had opened in Santa Maria, and when he returned, John started taking classes. It was not long before John was helping with the kids' classes.

"Eventually, I was running kids' programs and I got good at it," John said. "You can't control them. Kids do whatever the hell they want, and sometimes I wouldn't know what to do, but the kids taught me how to be a good teacher."

John quoted the British poet William Wordsworth.

"The child is the father of the man."

"I treat them how I should have been treated," John said. "I went through all my shit—I joke that I was raised by wolves—so I could learn what it takes to interact with these kids in a healthy way that really benefits them."

John's success as a teacher came easy because he gives the kids everything he needed but never got as a child. John quoted Frederick Douglass who said, "It's easier to build strong children than to repair broken men."

"When there's a kid who's losing their shit, sometimes they just need a hug and somebody to sit down and listen," John said. "When I was a kid, I was told to go away. I'm able to provide what a lot of kids need—acceptance."

John explained that although teaching kids is rewarding, it's not always easy.

"It's literally the most fulfilling thing I've ever done," John said. "Don't get me wrong, there are days when I wonder, am I fit to parent today? Am I fit to be somebody's mentor? Not always, but even if I'm having a tough day, I always ask what I can do right now to want to be in this kid's life?"

There have been times when John has considered quitting Jiu-Jitsu.

"At times, it was kind of hard to swallow," John said. "I've reached points where my body was broken, and I was overworked, underpaid, and felt unappreciated. It's really hard to find self-worth living like that, but I dedicated my life to Jiu-Jitsu, no matter what the outcome, because I owe everything to the art."

Jiu-Jitsu has become much more than a hobby for John.

"If I'm going to survive and have a good life, I have to do this," John said. "If I didn't have Jiu-Jitsu to calm my nerves, I'd be fucked up because there's way too much going on in my head."

When John realized how much Jiu-Jitsu benefited him, he committed to doing it for the rest of his life.

"After a lot of injuries, it's hard getting out of bed," John said. "But I just put my head down and keep moving forward."

It's because of these struggles that John said every kid, and every man, needs to learn how to fight.

"It wasn't until after I learned how to fight that I realized how much I needed to," John said. "Because life is a fight."

John said hard times are what build character, and he quoted Rumi: "You have to keep breaking your heart until it opens."

There was a time when John despised religion or spirituality, but the opportunity to open his own Jiu-Jitsu school has caused him to reconsider.

"For a long time, I thought about running a school in Arroyo Grande," John said. "So, when the chance came, it was like the law of attraction, without all the hippie bullshit."

Through the years, John has felt internal conflict every time he has had to change schools because he feels loyalty to everyone who has taught him.

"I will always be grateful to the people who taught me Jiu-Jitsu," John said. "After a while, you realize you're on your own, especially when you get injured. Other people care, but ultimately it's up to me to care for myself."

John has accepted that he is ultimately responsible for his own success.

"Most people seek external fulfillment," John said. "I don't care about being rich, but I don't want to be homeless either. Internal fulfillment is more important to me now. I know what I need to do for myself. I need to embody Jiu-Jitsu and share it with others. No matter what, if I work toward that, I will be fulfilled internally."

Mahamed Aly

When Mahamed Aly left Rio de Janeiro, he walked away from almost everything—his home, friends, family, and training partners—but he brought with him his determination to becoming a world champion.

"It was rough, man," Mahamed said. "I could not communicate because I didn't speak English, and the people were cold. It was different in Brazil, because kids were running in the streets, and making friends comes naturally when you're young."

The weekends in the U.S. were especially rough for Mahamed when he looked at social media and saw his friends in Brazil having fun without him.

"I would be alone the whole weekend," Mahamed said. "But I did not have a plan B. My two options were to win or win. There were times I would cry at home because I was so lonely, but I didn't have an option to quit. There was no other way. I had to keep going."

That was the beginning of a four-year journey of intense training and competition that earned Mahamed world championship titles at purple and brown belt levels as he worked his way to the black belt division. When he finally reached the final seconds of the last black belt match of the world championships, Mahamed struggled to process what had just happened.

"At first, I did not understand what was going on," Mahamed said. "Then I realized, 'Oh, shit, I just won the worlds.' I had been thinking about that for ten years, then suddenly, I got it. The only thing I can compare it to is the day my daughter was born. I don't think the same way now, but in that moment, I felt like I could have died and I'd have been happy."

Mahamed started Jiu-Jitsu when he was 15 years old. At that time, he never thought about winning championships. He had a lot of energy as a kid and was just looking for something fun to do. He tried kickboxing for a few months until a friend, who also did kickboxing, invited Mahamed to try MMA.

"I said, 'Sure,'" Mahamed said when his friend asked him to roll, "because in my mind, I could beat this guy in kickboxing, so I thought I could beat him in whatever we did. Then he got me in a triangle choke, and I didn't know what to do. That's when I started training Jiu-Jitsu."

Mahamed grew to love Jiu-Jitsu, but he kept training with no visions of becoming great.

"To be honest, I didn't want to beat people. I just wanted to not get beat," Mahamed said. "Then I started to learn how to defend, and every day I learned one new thing. Step-by-step, I got better. Then one day I won, then lost, and won again. I never wanted to be a legend. I just wanted to keep getting better and doing my thing."

What began as an idle pastime eventually became Mahamed's passion.

"I keep my demons away by doing Jiu-Jitsu," Mahamed said.

"When I found Jiu-Jitsu, for two or three hours a day, I would not think about violence or people doing bad shit. I would just think about improving. That's where I found peace in my life."

The poverty-stricken favelas of Brazil are very different from the U.S.

"I grew up in a very rough environment," Mahamed said. "We would get one pair of shoes at Christmas, but my feet would grow, and I was stuck with those shoes the entire year. I wore the same grass-stained shoes to school, sports, and parties."

Being poor was the only thing Mahamed knew, but poverty also came with more tragic consequences.

"If you don't see people dying, death is a fear," Mahamed said. "But when you see people dying, it's a reality. I lived that reality."

Mahamed saw lots of death at a very young age because of the crime and drugs in Rio's favelas.

"My friend that introduced me to Jiu-Jitsu was a pretty talented kid, but he was doing stupid shit," Mahamed said. "He won all the Jiu-Jitsu and Muy Thai tournaments, but he also tried to steal a bus. A cop was there and shot and killed him."

Mahamed did not like the environment he grew up in, but he did not know anything else.

"When I was nine, my dad was killed and left in the road," Mahamed said. "We don't know exactly what happened, but my dad was a chauffeur, and it looks like somebody killed him to steal his car."

It was devastating for Mahamed to lose his father at such a young age, but that also triggered a series of other challenges.

"It wasn't just losing my dad," Mahamed said. "Because when my dad died, I also lost my friends, my home, my privacy—basically, I lost everything."

Mahamed's mother and father had purchased the new car one week before it was stolen. Without her husband's income, Mahamed's mother was forced to sell their small home to pay off the loan for the new car that was stolen. That forced their family to move in with family members in another city.

"It was rough for all of us," Mahamed said. "I was nine and didn't have a dad anymore. My mom had to leave for work at 7:00 a.m. and came back at 9:00 p.m. We would be at home all day by ourselves learning how to live and protect ourselves. I had to work and try to make money. I had to become the man in the family because I didn't have any other option."

Mahamed explained that his reality was like that of most of the kids in Brazil.

"Brazil is kind of different than America," Mahamed said. "I don't know why, but most kids in Brazil don't have a dad. At 13 years old, kids already have their own kids. They're not adults in age, but they have adult responsibilities."

All these bad things happened to Mahamed, but he never felt sorry for himself. He was too distracted trying to survive.

"I wanted to get out of there, but I didn't know how," Mahamed said. "I just didn't want to die there."

One day, former UFC light heavyweight champion Vitor Belfort showed up at the gym and struck up a conversation with Mahamed. Vitor commented on Mahamed's size and skill and was surprised that he was only a 15-year-old blue belt. When Vitor learned that Mahamed wanted to fight in MMA, Vitor invited him to Las Vegas for his next fight.

That conversation led to Mahamed connecting with the legendary Nogueira brothers. Eventually, Mahamed left his mother's home and moved into the Nogueira fight team's house and began training for professional cage fights.

"It was awesome," Mahamed said, "because for the first time in my life I was training with people who were bigger than me. I also got to see that famous people are people just like us."

Mahamed respected the way guys like Rodrigo "Minotauro" Nogueira, a former UFC and Pride champion, carried themselves and treated people.

"He's super famous," Mahamed said, "but he treated people right. Those guys walk around the gym with bare feet. They don't care about expensive stuff, because they just want to keep improving."

Mahamed was reluctant to say it, but he admired how humble the Nogueiras were.

"I don't like the word humble," Mahamed said. "I think humble is when you think you're just like everybody else, and I don't think that's true. When I'm fighting, I don't see myself like other people. I don't want to be average, ever. When I say that, some people get offended, they think I'm cocky, but if you want to be a world champion, you can't believe that everyone is just like you."

Mahamed explained that outside the competition mats, he feels differently; but as a high-level competitor, he's dedicated to becoming the best he can.

For Mahamed to get to the U.S., he had to step outside his comfort zone.

"I'm still very shy," Mahamed said. "I don't know about Americans, but in Brazil, there are a lot of hungry people. When people are hungry, if somebody comes out with food, everyone jumps on the food because they're trying to eat to survive. I realized that every time an opportunity would show up, I would be the last one to get it because I was shy. I was afraid of people, so I just shut my mouth."

Mahamed could not get to the U.S. on his own, but he was not confident enough to share his goals with the people who could help him achieve them. Jiu-Jitsu helped Mahamed develop courage that enabled him to overcome his introversion.

"I didn't have money to pay for the world championships," Mahamed said, "but I would not ask anybody because I was too shy. People saw that I was dedicated, and they wanted to help, so I had to learn to say thank you and show appreciation."

Eventually, Mahamed's instructors started asking him to lead portions of classes, and that forced him to talk in front of the group.

"That's how it started," Mahamed said. "That's when I forced myself to learn to talk to people."

It took Mahamed a couple of tries before his U.S. visa was approved, but eventually he competed in his first world championship in the U.S.

"It was a crazy experience. I didn't have money, so I never thought I'd be able to go to the U.S. to compete in the worlds," Mahamed said. "I made it to the semifinals, but with thirty seconds left, I lost my focus. I lost, but it was a great experience because I fought really well."

On this trip, Mahamed met Lloyd Irvin, and not long afterward, Lloyd helped Mahamed move to the U.S., where he joined their fight team.

"He's a great guy and has helped me a lot," Mahamed said. "He's very focused, and when he wants something, he's going to do everything to get it, just like me. As a coach, he wanted a black belt world title, so he would wake up every day and work for it, and it paid off."

Mahamed explained what he believes separates those who achieve high levels and those who don't.

"Desire is not enough," Mahamed said. "It's more about discipline than desire. Many people want to do a lot of things, but they don't have the discipline to do what it takes."

Mahamed believes that he was disciplined in Jiu-Jitsu because of how much he loves the sport.

"I'm not disciplined to do anything else," Mahamed said. "I did shitty in school because I did not value education. I didn't want to sit in class and read, and when you don't appreciate it, there's no love. Without love, there's no passion, but when you find something you love, you're willing to overcome all obstacles."

Mahamed compared Jiu-Jitsu to raising kids. Raising children is hard, but because you love them, you're willing to do whatever it takes.

The discipline that brought Mahamed to a world championship also came with some pain.

"I went through two years of pure stress in my life," Mahamed said. "It became stressful when it became my job. When I started winning, I didn't want to lose, and the more I won, the more stressed I became. I wanted to make everything perfect. I wanted to be the best. When I won, I didn't celebrate my victories, because in my mind, I was already the best. I was supposed to win. When I lost, I felt like a piece of shit and life became miserable."

Mahamed noticed that he was living the same life as the regular guy who goes to work every day and hates his job. What used to be his love and passion had become hell.

"I think you should try to be the best you can," Mahamed said, "but it's a problem when you're obsessed about perfection. We all know that perfection doesn't exist, but we keep looking for it until one day you wake up and realize you're living a miserable life."

Mahamed is grateful for the success he has had and is excited about continuing to excel in Jiu-Jitsu competition, but now he hopes to also use Jiu-Jitsu for something bigger than himself.

"Because I came from a very rough background, I've always wanted to give back," Mahamed said. "When I moved to the United States, I felt selfish. I felt like I was doing all of it for me. I've always wanted to do more for others, but I wasn't in a position to do so, but now I'm getting there. Now the goal is bigger than me. I want to make people's lives better by giving back to the kids in Brazil. That's the way I approach life now."

Nicolas Gregoriades

Nicolas Gregoriades left his home in South Africa and arrived in London with only a couple of hundred bucks in his pocket. After trying another gym, he eventually discovered Roger Gracie's Jiu-Jitsu academy.

When Nicolas knocked on the door, a tall but unassuming kid answered. "This guy doesn't look tough at all," Nicolas thought.

"He looked like a regular dude," Nicolas said. "He had that foppish haircut and was kind of pale. I thought these crazy fighters were supposed to be tan, Mediterranean-looking guys."

Nicolas had some no-gi grappling experience and had been submitting a lot of guys at home with kneebars. One of his friends knew of Roger Gracie and heard Nicolas was visiting the academy.

"If you kneebar that guy, I will call you 'sir' for the rest of your life," his friend said.

"My kneebars are amazing," the overly confident, 20-year-old Nicolas said to his friend. "Jiu-Jitsu guys don't know kneebars."

Roger was gracious and welcomed Nicolas into the gym during their lunchtime class.

"I'll never forget that day," Nicolas said. "There were only four guys in class, so I asked if I could spar with him."

That was the beginning of Nicolas' four-and-a-half-year journey to becoming Roger Gracie's first black belt. Since then, Nicolas has taught Jiu-Jitsu seminars around the world, founded the online community and podcast *The Jiu-Jitsu Brotherhood*, built the online *Master Academy*, authored two Jiu-Jitsu books, and produced multiple video training products.

"I look back at that decision to train with Roger as one of those pivotal moments in my life," Nicolas said. "Things could have been very different if I hadn't knocked on that door that day."

Nicolas had never heard much about Roger, but after they rolled together, Nicolas knew he had discovered someone special.

"In the ignorance of youth, I thought I was a tough guy," Nicolas said. "I was good at this grappling thing, but he smashed me. I mean, he totally smashed me and made it look effortless. I was super-excited because I could see the potential if I could get anywhere near that good."

Before he met Roger, Nicolas had left his family's home in Cape Town, South Africa, for London—a common destination for young people from former British colonies like South Africa, New Zealand, and Australia.

"In Cape Town, I felt like a big fish in a small pond," Nicolas said. "You know that expression, 'In the land of the blind, the one-eyed man is king.' Back in those days, a visiting purple belt in South Africa was a big occasion. I needed to expand my horizons if I wanted to progress."

As far back as Nicolas can remember, he was fascinated by martial arts. His father was a karate black belt, and Nicolas can remember sitting on the sidelines as a young boy, watching his father's class.

"I remember thinking, 'Wow, this is amazing. My dad is a super-hero,'" Nicolas said.

At seven years old, Nicolas started taking a judo class.

"I absolutely loved it, but I was kind of disappointed we weren't striking," Nicolas said. "At that age, you watch all the movies and think the best martial artists can kill a dude with a one-inch punch. Little did I know, judo was one of the best things that could have happened, because later my Jiu-Jitsu development accelerated from the grappling I learned in judo."

Nicolas took a break from martial arts during his teen years, but after high school he began dabbling in boxing until a friend told him about a cage-fighting gym.

"I was a young dude, and I wanted to know the best stuff," Nicolas said. "I wanted to know how to be the most dangerous guy I could be."

Nicolas and his brother went to a class taught by a man who had done a little training with the legend, Rickson Gracie.

"He was this Yoda-type gentleman who taught himself the basic principles and the science behind fighting," Nicolas said. "He had been a fourth-degree karate black belt, but he renounced his belt when he realized it was a highly dysfunctional art."

At the end of that cage-fighting class, Nicolas was paired up with another new student.

"He taught us the rear naked choke," Nicolas said, "and when we sparred, I strangled that guy so easily. *This stuff works.* I had to learn it."

Nicolas trained there for a couple of years and then opened his own grappling club.

"I was a 20-year-old kid who thought he knew it all," Nicolas said. "But once I graduated college, I wanted to leave South Africa. I realized that I couldn't develop the way I wanted to without leaving to expand my horizons."

Nicolas began training in London before Roger Gracie was recognized as one of the best fighters in the world.

"I often think how different my life would have been if I'd gone to another gym," Nicolas said. "It wasn't until later that I realized just how incredibly lucky I was to have stumbled upon this gem. Roger let me train for free when he hardly knew me, and I doubt there would have been another gym that would have done that. I'll never forget it."

When Nicolas arrived in London, he was in excellent physical condition and knew the fundamentals of grappling. He was submitting many of the students at Roger's school, so within a few weeks, Roger awarded Nicolas his blue belt. Before long, he was teaching other students in private lessons.

Nicolas' life was consumed with Jiu-Jitsu. He lived next door to the academy and spent five to six hours training and teaching every day.

"That was the first time in my life that I understood the power of focus," Nicolas said. "Focused will and focused intent were the greatest gifts I discovered during that period. Jiu-Jitsu was my focus. There was nothing else. I wasn't there to party, and I wasn't there to make money. I was there to get my black belt in Jiu-Jitsu."

Nicolas credits that focus and teaching for his rapid progress.

"Learning and teaching, together, create a recipe for something very special," Nicolas said. "They're synergistic, and when taken together there's an exponential increase in retention. It's greater than the sum of its parts."

Nicolas attended three to four classes a week, and then taught what he had learned to students during his private lessons.

"It was almost like an incubator," Nicolas said. "If I attended Roger's class on Friday, I'd have four back-to-back private students on Saturday to teach what I'd just learned. I'd be able to revise and consolidate those techniques with four hours of teaching to reinforce that knowledge."

Nicolas said that Jiu-Jitsu students are typically shown a handful of techniques in a class and then return a couple of days later to do a completely different set.

"The retention is so low because they've only had one exposure to it," Nicolas said. "I really want students to review as much as possible. At the end of every one of my classes, there is always review. Then a couple of days later we'll review the material again. I'm trying to recreate that forced review that I went through."

After only four and a half years of training in London, Nicolas was awarded his black belt by Roger Gracie.

"I'm happy to be a Jiu-Jitsu black belt," Nicolas said. "Goddamn, it sounds clichéd, but it was the journey that was special."

After earning his belt, Nicolas' perspective on goals began to change.

"I'm embarrassed to say that I just wanted that belt," Nicolas said. "I wish it was something deeper than that, but I just wanted to be a black belt."

Author and Jiu-Jitsu black belt Roy Dean had once told Nicolas, "As a man, you are constantly paying your dues."

"That struck me to my core," Nicolas said. "I'd always thought that there was a destination in life that you arrived at, and once you got there, you could check that box, and you were done."

Nicolas explained that once you get in shape, find a good wife, or build a successful business, it's tempting to think you can take your foot off the gas.

"With the black belt, I thought I was done because I'd reached the top of the mountain," Nicolas said. "But today I realize that anything you achieve is not the destination. It's a continuous journey. You have to continuously hone, refine, and keep progressing, otherwise it decays. The journey never ends."

That said, Nicolas recognizes there is an objective element to Jiu-Jitsu belts that inspires students to keep training.

"Most purple belts can beat blue belts, and brown belts can beat purple belts," Nicolas said. "Having that measurement is motivating for people because you get an indicator of your progress. Whether people like it or not, it's one of the reasons Jiu-Jitsu academies are more popular than no-gi academies."

As an entrepreneur, Nicolas is learning that most people have it wrong when they chase money. Instead they should try to provide as much value as possible, and the money will follow. Jiu-Jitsu is similar.

"I think I would've progressed even more quickly if I didn't chase the belt," Nicolas said. "I should have focused more on the lessons and how much fun I was having hanging out with cool dudes while we learn to strangle people."

With years to reflect on these experiences, Nicolas has a better understanding of what drove him to chase that belt with such vigor.

"I realize that a large part of my journey in trying to be this stronger, tougher guy was because I wanted the approval of my father," Nicolas said. "My father is a very 'alpha' dude, but I was a little bit of a nerdy kid that loved to read. I always thought he would have been happier if he'd had a son who was like the quarterback on the football team."

Nicolas was not gifted with athleticism, but there are many fighters he's trained with that are blessed with athletic talent. Nicolas recalled one of his training partners who could have eaten jelly beans and watched TV all day and still remained in great shape. During one of their training sessions, his partner commented on Nicolas' strength.

"God might have made you, but I made me," Nicolas told him. "When it comes to athleticism, I fucking bled for that. I started with less, but I worked on it more."

Nicolas said there's a difference between talent and skill.

"Talent is a fickle mistress," Nicolas said. "Talent can come and go, but skill is something you earn control over."

Nicolas had a decent childhood, but the relationship with his father was strained.

"My father was quite hard on me," Nicolas said. "He always held back approval, but in hindsight, I'm glad he did. It drove me to work out like an animal, and eventually I became athletic. I became physical. I became what my dad respected."

One day, Nicolas received a letter from his father confessing how he felt about his children.

"I look at you and your brother, and I'm so proud of you," the letter said. "You boys are everything I wanted to be when I was your age."

"If he had sent that to me five years earlier, it would have been like the sun shining upon my face," Nicolas said. "But the funny thing is that once my dad was ready to finally give me his approval, I no longer needed it."

When Nicolas was a kid, his dad was his hero. But as Nicolas grew up, he discovered that his father had a very difficult childhood of his own and was a man with flaws like everyone else.

"I think most others that have been through what my father went through wouldn't have even tried," Nicolas said. "He definitely tried his best, and I'm thankful for everything that led to this point. I definitely had resentment, but I'm at peace with it now."

Nicolas' mother had a very different effect on his ambition.

"My mom made me feel like I could do anything," Nicolas said. "I don't necessarily know whether that was true, but it has never left me."

Nicolas recalled a time in elementary school when he ranked fifth academically out of the 38 students in his class.

"This is totally unacceptable," Nicolas' mother said when he got home. "You and I both know you should've come in first."

In contrast to the relationship with his father, Nicolas was not seeking approval from his mother.

"It was more that she instilled a belief that I had this thing, and I should not waste it," Nicolas said. "Trying to live up to the impossible standard my mom set made life difficult, but in the back of my mind, I believe that if I can do anything I want, then I should want to be something really good."

Through a lot of self-reflection Nicolas began to understand some of what had been driving him, but there was still a void that he could not figure out.

"I wasn't a down-and-out dude or anything like that," Nicolas said. "I had good friends and I could make decent money teaching Jiu-Jitsu. I just felt there was something missing. I hit a point where my mind was torturing me. Every morning I'd wake up and my mind would find the thought that would cause me the most pain and just start whipping me with it over and over again."

Nicolas pushed on as he tried to think his way through it.

"My mind was not my friend," Nicolas said. "I always thought my mind was my greatest ally. It was my weapon. It had always helped me solve problems and get what I wanted, but I realized this thing was out of control. The mind is a wonderful servant but a terrible master, and at that point my mind was the master of me."

Nicolas turned to meditation, which helped him quiet the chatter in his mind.

"Meditation was the crack that started the flood of desire to dive deeper," Nicolas said. "I wanted to become the best human I could be. I wanted to become a person worthy of the black belt, instead of just wanting the belt."

Nicolas watched a documentary about ayahuasca, a brew made

from the bark of a tropical vine that is traditionally used in spiritual medicine ceremonies with indigenous people of the Amazon.

"I just kept lying awake, thinking about it," Nicolas said. "There was just something not right. It was this itch that could not be scratched. There's something missing, and life wasn't what I wanted it to be."

Eventually Nicolas decided to see if he could find the answers he was seeking with ayahuasca.

"I thought if I could take something that pulls back the veil and allows me to dive to the root of my psyche, I might find the splinter and be able to dig it out," Nicolas said.

When he drank the shot-sized glass of medicine, he lay on the ground until it finally began to kick in. Then he started to freak out.

"Anyone who's done ayahuasca knows that the true growth happens when you surrender and let it do what it needs to do," Nicolas said. "It's difficult to describe because it was such a foreign experience. It took me to a depth so deep within, it was beyond anything I was prepared for."

The gift of ayahuasca was that it took Nicolas beyond the ego and conscious thought.

"Ego is a defense mechanism," Nicolas said. "We develop it to create boundaries that keep us safe. The ego serves a purpose, but it in many instances it can become unhealthy."

Nicolas described ayahuasca as a virtual teacher that cuts through the ego and showed him the root of all fears and neuroses.

"My biggest fear is not living up to my full potential," Nicolas said. "Every boy, whether he knows it or not, craves his father's approval. It's one of the reasons that many segments of our societies are fucked up. In households where there is no father figure, it causes a huge psychic gap in boys and they try to fill that any way they can."

But ayahuasca took him to a level beyond those conscious fears.

"It took me straight to my deepest layer," Nicolas said. "Ayahuasca was trying to show me that one day I'm going to die. That is the root underneath everything. If you're afraid of a snake, it's not the snake you fear, it's that you're afraid of dying by the snake."

Nicolas began to understand that we all eventually return to nature, and it felt peaceful from that perspective.

"After ayahuasca, it was almost like this brake had been released," Nicolas said. "It started with a desire to get my father's approval, but when I realized I no longer needed it, I stopped hero worship, including my dad, Jiu-Jitsu teachers, celebrities, or anyone. I no longer require the approval of anyone except myself. And when I dug deep enough into my fears, I realized that the worst that could ultimately happen was that I die. Once I began to understand that death is not something to fear, it gave me the courage to try anything, because everything else is insignificant when compared to death."

Ricardo Liborio

When Ricardo Liborio's youngest daughter was 1½ years old, she spent three months in the hospital and 15 days in the intensive care unit. Doctors discovered that the soft part of her head had fused together before her brain was fully developed. As her brain developed, it compressed the optic nerve against the skull, which left her permanently blind.

Ricardo's daughter endured two complicated brain surgeries, with doctors breaking open her skull to allow room for her brain to grow. After the second surgery, she started having seizures.

"It was a rough time," Ricardo said. "I have two pictures in my wallet from when we were in the ICU and my wife and I had to learn to sleep in the chairs. Every time something goes wrong in life, I think about that time. It gives me perspective."

Ricardo recalled being in the cafeteria of the Miami Children's Hospital's neurology wing at 2:00 in the morning with three other fathers.

"I talked to these guys every night for three months," Ricardo said. "I was worried that my daughter was going to be blind, but all three of their kids had brain cancer. Two of them died, and I felt so sorry for their families, but it gave me perspective. My daughter was blind, but when you see what I saw, you think, 'This sucks,' but you lived through it."

This experience was the toughest challenge in Ricardo's life, but it was through Jiu-Jitsu that he learned how to cope with this kind of adversity.

Ricardo Liborio is a black belt under Carlson Gracie. He was a gold medalist at the first World Jiu-Jitsu Championships in Brazil, and he won an Abu Dhabi Combat Club World Championship Superfight. Ricardo is a founder of two of the most successful mixed martial teams in history—Brazilian Top Team and American Top Team. He was also a coach in the *Ultimate Fighter* reality television show.

* * *

"Enduring your own pain is one thing," Ricardo said, "but when something happens to your family, that hits you at a different level. I lived through that terrible time when I learned that my daughter was blind. I didn't know what to do, but I thought a lot about what I learned from Carlson and competition.

"There will be setbacks, there will be walls, and there will be bumps in the road. There is no way you're going to pass through life without facing adversity. Through competition I realized that the most important thing is to keep going. You don't have to like it, but you can't quit."

Ricardo broke a rib while fighting in one of the ADCC tournaments. Doctors gave him a cortisone shot to help him continue, but he was still suffering.

"It was really too much pain, but I continued," Ricardo said. "I was ashamed I lost, because I really thought I could have won. I took third place, but it was not good enough for me. I wanted to be the best, and I wanted to impress Carson, but I felt like I failed.

"Carlson could read people so well. He was like a skilled psychologist, and if he thought you could handle it, he would push, but if you were down, he knew just what to say. He knew when to push and when to pull."

After Ricardo's disappointing third-place finish at ADCC, Carlson supported Ricardo by reminding him that it was good he did not enjoy losing, but the only thing that mattered was that he kept going.

"Carlson was there for me even though I was wearing the bronze," Ricardo said. "Of course, everybody enjoys first place, but that wasn't what mattered. He cared more about the person than the championship. He had his own style—he could be tough—but he was also kind-hearted and loved to help people."

Ricardo has made a career of training some of the best professional fighters in the world. In that business, there is a lot of pressure to focus on the winners and ignore everyone else.

"I've never been that kind of a coach." Ricardo said. "I understand the pressure of professional teams. Not everyone is going to be a champion, but they are still beautiful people and I'm not going to quit on them."

Ricardo explained that coaching is different from mentoring. With fight technology constantly evolving, there is no way any coach can keep up with all the latest techniques.

"The most important thing I learned from Carlson, which I've tried to mimic, is that you have to care," Ricardo said. "Carlson was not the most technical fighter, but he created the right environment, and that's the most important thing."

That supportive environment allowed Ricardo to take risks that allowed him to grow.

"If you had a bad competition on the weekend, you come back on Monday and just keep working. That's where you grow in martial arts," he explained. "If you put everything into winning, and you lose, are you going to quit? Then what will you do when life gets tough? But you can develop a champion's mentality, and that's what will keep you going when you hit life's darkest moments."

After years of competition, Ricardo focused on coaching fighters. He was struggling with severe pain from injuries, and it was challenging to focus on his fighters while he was also competing. He needed to focus on one or the other.

"When I was coaching, I was dedicated to the business," Ricardo said. "As you get older, you don't think about competition as much as you think about being involved in something you enjoy. I started finding teaching more interesting than my own training, and I didn't want to miss coaching my guys the next day because I was in pain from training. I took a lot of time away from competition, but I missed it so much."

When Ricardo was almost 50, he received a call from ADCC, inviting him to fight in a superfight against Mario Sperry, his friend and former teammate from Brazilian Top Team.

"It was such an honor," Ricardo said. "I know how good he is. He's a beast. He's a champion, but what's the worst that could happen, I get submitted in 20 seconds? That would have been worth it because of the experience I had training for the fight."

After 14 years since his last competition, Ricardo went to the doctor to help him manage his neck and back injuries. When he was physically ready, he took a year away from coaching to train for the match.

"I had to put my ego aside," Ricardo said. "Every day I was training with guys half my age, and I got my ass beat, but it was really good for me. I was not doing it for the medals. I was there for the journey. I needed that to get myself healthy and motivated. It's great that I won, but even if I had lost, it was worth spending time training with the guys. The brotherhood—it was so amazing. It was such a privilege."

After that superfight, Ricardo moved on to the next chapter of his life.

"I am not in competition mode right now," Ricardo said. "I'm not focused on medals, trophies, and winning. I respect that, and I was part of that world for a long time, but only 3 percent of martial arts students are competitors. What about the other 97 percent?

"Competition and trophies are really cool, but it gets much deeper than just a medal. I see Jiu-Jitsu as a tool that can help all people, no matter what race, gender, sexuality, or religion. Jiu-Jitsu is like therapy. It's the new yoga. Jiu-Jitsu is the yoga for tough people."

Ricardo is concerned that championships, medals, fame, and money receive more attention than the personal growth that comes from martial arts.

"I understand the fight business," Ricardo said. "I was there since the beginning. I'm one of the few guys who was involved in the sport before it was called MMA. It was Vale Tudo and No Holds Barred. I lived in this circus for quite a while. I saw the shift as they kept squeezing lemons, trying to get more money and viewers out of the fighters.

"Everything revolves around how much attention you can get it. If you're the worst of the worst character but you can trash talk, you'll make more money, but at the same time you'll inspire a whole generation of young people to mimic a blueprint that brings a worse society. That's just not right.

"I understand that money is dictating the shift. Money follows what the people support, but that is the opposite of what I believe the martial arts are about. How is it going to be with a community full of aggressive trash-talking gangs? I'm not saying we should raise a bunch of pussies, but the purpose of martial arts is self-defense. You get yourself ready for anything, but that doesn't mean you should become an aggressive bully."

Ricardo believes the 97 percent will receive more benefit from martial arts than the 3 percent. The non-athlete who takes up Jiu-Jitsu will experience more growth in confidence and in physical and mental health than the champion does when he wins the next tournament.

"It's therapeutic every time you are preparing to become a better self tomorrow," Ricardo said. "If you're living through a storm in your mind, when you step into a Jiu-Jitsu session, you stop thinking. The problem is when people use drinking, drugs, and sex as a tool to escape. I'm not a saint either, but there's healthier ways to take a break."

To expand the reach of the benefits of Jiu-Jitsu, Ricardo is heading up a new program at the University of Central Florida.

"I'm the head Brazilian Jiu-Jitsu coach at UCF," Ricardo said. "I think I'm teaching the first two-credit Brazilian Jiu-Jitsu college course. UCF is the second-largest university in the United States, with 66,000 kids."

With that university's large population, there is an opportunity to touch a lot of people through the benefits of Jiu-Jitsu.

"We are creating a holistic curriculum," Ricardo said. "The students are learning about Brazil, Carlson Gracie, and some of the Jiu-Jitsu culture. We are going to have music and barbecues. I'm trying to pass some of my culture to the American kids in the universities. This is my mission today. It's something I'm good at, and I think I can contribute so much. The reality is, the more people you can help create healthy habits, the better our world becomes. I know that sounds like bullshit, but it's not. I really, truly think this way."

The success of this program will come from creating the right atmosphere.

"It's got to be a good environment," Ricardo said. "Although competition taught me a lot of things, it's not just about competing. It's about learning character and a moral code. Character development comes from being part of a good environment that has meaning. That environment requires the right person who welcomes you into the sport and cares about you as a person instead of your medals."

Ricardo does not measure success by his finances, but rather by the impact he can have on people through Jiu-Jitsu.

"Success comes from the amount of people I can touch and make feel better about themselves," Ricardo said. "I love the martial arts. This sport has given me everything, so if I can give that to others, I will be successful."

Roy Dean

A t 16 years old, Roy Dean felt trapped in Anchorage, Alaska, so he left home for Japan as part of an exchange student program. When he arrived at his new high school, students were required to study one of the traditional Japanese arts, such as fencing (kendo), archery (kyudo), or floral arrangements (ikebana).

"Steven Seagal was popular at that time," Roy said. "I was interested in aikido because I wanted to be able to take on five guys in a pool hall."

Aikido was not available at his Japanese high school, but judo was an available art option.

"Initially, I wasn't that pleased," Roy said, "but judo changed the entire trajectory of my life."

The judo program was conservative, so Roy was not allowed to wear a uniform until he first learned how to fall properly (ukemi).

"Judo is very tough," Roy said. "I did hundreds, if not thousands, of hard break falls and ended up with huge bruises on my shoulders."

After six weeks of falling drills, Roy was finally allowed on the mats and given the opportunity to spar with the judo team captain.

"No matter what I did, within seconds I was on the ground, looking up at the ceiling," Roy said. "I would attack him again, and boom, like it was nothing. He must have thrown me at least 15 times in a couple of minutes."

Roy was completely outclassed by the smaller and weaker team captain, but Roy was inspired.

"It was electrifying," Roy said. "He was small and not intimidating at all. If I could do what he just did to me, no one would be able to mess with me. I wanted that same power. It was mind-blowing."

A lot of Westerners romanticize martial arts in the East, but that experience taught Roy the secret behind the mysticism.

"I've had a fascination with Japan, but I learned that it's just doing a lot of repetitions," Roy said. "It's a lot of shutting your mouth and being able to eat the pain. If you do that long enough, one day your body responds without thinking and you're able to achieve amazing things."

From that initial exposure to judo, Roy has been on a lifelong journey as a martial artist. He is a third-degree Brazilian Jiu-Jitsu black belt as well as a black belt in judo and aikido. Roy has taught thousands of students around the world through his seminars and videos. Roy is also an author of two books that document his martial arts journey, *The Martial Apprentice* and *Becoming the Black Belt*.

* * *

Growing up in Alaska required that Roy develop a level of toughness that many outsiders never experience. Roy attended a multicultural high school in Alaska, where the population is more ethnically diverse than an outsider might think.

"People would fight in high school," Roy said, "but it wasn't

South Central LA. It was one of the few places in the country with no Bloods or Crips. Everyone there, whether you were a janitor or a doctor, had to deal with the elements, so we were united against the weather."

People were down to earth in Anchorage out of necessity. It was hard to be pretentious when New York fashions were gratefully traded in for North Face jackets and heavy boots.

"But there were some tough guys up there," Roy said. "Especially with the military bases. Those guys were always into martial arts."

Roy grew up with both of his parents, who raised Roy in their later years. Roy's father was two generations older than he was.

"My father was with me, but he was distant," Roy said. "He joined the Marines when he was 17 and went to the South Pacific to fight in World War II. My father was a Marine, with a crew cut, until the day he died."

Roy's father was from the generation in which a man's role was to provide for the family, so instead of taking Roy to organized sports, his father spent his free time at the American Legion post.

"That was his place; it was where he bonded with his fellow warriors," Roy said. "I see that in myself. I don't go to a bar, but I go to an academy to rub shoulders with young and old warriors."

Roy understands his father's role, but it created a void in his younger years.

"My father was so distant that I lacked a male role model to emulate," Roy said. "That was part of the appeal of going to Japan. I was seeking new experiences and adventures, or that next level in my life."

After spending a year in Japan studying judo, Roy went to Ontario, Canada, to finish high school. While in Toronto, he encountered a man confining a woman in the subway entrance.

"She was clearly distressed," Roy said. "Her back was pinned against the wall and she was squirming to get away. I had a black belt in judo, but I still didn't know what to do. I wanted to have the capacity to help her, but I did not feel qualified, and that stuck with me for a long time."

After finishing high school, Roy continued his journey as a martial artist. He moved to Monterey, California, to pursue his earlier interest in aikido and Aiki-jujutsu that had been inspired by the martial arts movies of the 1990s. Roy became a full-time, live-in apprentice under a Japanese jiujitsu and aikido master.

By this point, he had also seen Royce Gracie decimate his opponents in the UFC. With permission from his instructor, Roy began cross-training in Brazilian Jiu-Jitsu with Claudio Franca until Roy was accepted into the University of California, San Diego. The move to Southern California brought him to Jeet Kune Do and Brazilian Jiu-Jitsu instructor Roy Harris, who eventually awarded Roy his purple through third-degree black belts in BJJ.

After earning black belts in multiple arts, Roy gravitated to Brazilian Jiu-Jitsu.

"It's far more satisfying," Roy said. "Other systems don't really have the randori sparring method, and there is a 'martial truth' that is readily apparent when you tap in Brazilian Jiu-Jitsu."

Roy explained that in other martial arts, it's easy to dismiss a loss in training by saying, "Yeah, well, if you really attacked me, I could have done this or that."

"Nobody wastes their time saying that in Brazilian Jiu-Jitsu," Roy said, "Because Brazilian Jiu-Jitsu is the truth."

Roy graduated from UCSD with an ICAM (interdisciplinary computing and the arts major) degree.

"The programming classes were challenging," Roy said. "but what it ultimately taught me was how to teach myself, and that was time well spent."

To get through college, Roy learned how to find essential elements without getting bogged down in the minutiae. That was a skill that translated well into learning and teaching Jiu-Jitsu.

"If there are 21 elements of a triangle choke, what are the three key components?" Roy said. "What are three major moves that I can use to block the choke? Realizing that not everything has the same level of importance helps filter what matters most."

After college, Roy was hired as an audio engineer, where he did audio post-production and video editing. While working in that field, Roy realized he could blend his passion for martial arts with his career in media.

"I saw these full-time martial artists who were visiting my instructor, and I thought that was the life I wanted," Roy said. "They were making an enjoyable living without sitting in front of a computer in a windowless room for 10 hours a day."

Roy opened his own Jiu-Jitsu academy and used teaching and instructional DVDs as vehicles to share his art.

"If you look at it through a Brazilian lens, their ultimate celebration is competition and medals," Roy said. "But I came from a very different background. I came from a traditional Japanese jujutsu, judo, and aikido background, so I saw it through the lens of Jiu-Jitsu's historical evolution through the centuries."

Roy sees himself as an artist, but he said the art must come secondary to martial effectiveness.

"It's art through combat," Roy said. "You have to go through combat to transcend it into art. If you go the other way around, it's very difficult. You get to the art by getting good enough so that it looks smooth and artistic, but you have to pay your dues to be able to make it look like art. The most important thing is that you don't fool yourself."

When Roy was a young BJJ competitor, he realized that he was not aggressive enough in tournaments.

"I'm a nice guy," Roy said. "I wanted people to like me and respect my skill. I yearned to have the ability to dominate with minimal energy and perfect technique. I never wanted to roll too hard for fear of being a dick."

Roy explained that when people first learn Jiu-Jitsu, they are not "integrated into" their body. They do not have left/right or top/bottom symmetry. They are not sure what to do, so they just move with total body aggression.

"They just move forward," Roy said. "They don't know that reverse, left, and right are also very useful. You can continue to make progress, but you don't have to be locked in one direction."

A breakthrough came when Roy took a more clinical examination of the fight.

"What tripped the switch for me was getting to a point where I could be aggressive but without any emotion involved," Roy said. "There's almost a level of apathy with it. You don't care whether it works out. 'I am going to attack you, but I'm not emotionally invested in the attack.'"

Roy gave the example that when an opponent postures out of the triangle, he can switch to an arm lock.

"Attack without being attached, because with attachment comes emotion," Roy said. "If you want that triangle so badly, that's where you waste energy, because your mind is grasping for that thing you thought you wanted. Aggression leads to frustration."

Roy described fighting a 250-pound opponent who uses strength and aggression.

"I know what's not going to work," Roy said. "He's so big that I'm not going to sweep him. I have to climb or move around him. I don't have to get sucked into that game with guys who are forcing it."

When Roy was in the lower-belt levels, he would easily get caught in a battle of wills against stronger opponents, but it burned a lot of energy.

"Don't get sucked in" is Roy's inner dialogue when fighting these opponents. "Today, I have so many more pathways around these guys. They haven't explored those roads yet, but they're there. You just need to spend a little bit more time driving around the city. Then you can take the shortcuts."

The book *Power Versus Force* influenced Roy's thinking, and he adapted the ideas to Jiu-Jitsu. The book teaches that true power comes from within, but force is what people project onto others.

"You use all your strength to force the arm into the right position," Roy said. "Maybe you'll succeed, but maybe you won't. Power achieves the same end, but in a more graceful way. Instead of forcing the arm, you attack the neck, which forces the arm to come up and present itself for a spinning arm lock. You don't have to use that much energy. It's good timing based off what they gave you."

Roy said that when you begin learning Jiu-Jitsu it requires 100 percent effort to be effective, but as you gain more skill, you can begin to dial it back.

"I am at that point where I use Jiu-Jitsu like a finely tuned dimmer switch," Roy said. "You don't have to have it on all the way. As you get better, you can dial it back more and more. I will just match their light. If someone's shining way too bright and I don't feel like that today, I don't have to outshine them."

This is a distinction between Brazilian Jiu-Jitsu and many other martial arts.

"With the softer arts, you're dialing the dimmer switch up little by little," Roy said. "But then, if you meet someone who is at full brightness, you're just blown away because you don't have that capacity.

Instead, you have to be able to go to full brightness and then dim it back."

Jiu-Jitsu enables the fighter to accomplish the goal with less force, but Roy said that, as a man, you never stop paying your dues.

"It doesn't stop; you always have to learn more," Roy said. "You have to be a lifelong learner and adapt to the world that is constantly changing."

The lines became blurred when Roy's need for continual growth intersected with Jiu-Jitsu tournaments.

"I am a competitive person," Roy said. "But competition is a weird realm where you can get lost. The problem is people get addicted to chasing championships, and it can be an endless level of dissatisfaction. The only way you can win some games is to not participate."

Roy has won at the black-belt level, but he realized that to be a world champion black belt required another level of dedication.

"I was not near that level, nor was I willing to do everything you have to do to be a consistent contender. High level is still not that level. I knew my place and I learned to be comfortable there."

Roy enjoyed many years of competition, but as he grew, his passions also evolved. One of his earliest passions was music, and Brian Eno, one of the producers of the band U2, was influential to Roy's thinking.

"Brian Eno had the most amazing quote," Roy said. "When it came to pop music, Brian Eno said that most people try to hit the bull's-eye. But the bull's-eye is very crowded, so why don't you just make a new target?"

When Roy first launched his academy, people knew him as a good competitor, but they questioned whether he could be a good teacher. Later, when he was a well-respected teacher, people questioned why he did not compete.

"You go through different stages of the journey, but I've tried to keep making new targets," Roy said. "I went through that stage of hyper-competitiveness—whether that's in a tournament or in the dojo—and I feel like I've kind of graduated beyond that. Now I use Jiu-Jitsu to empower others, regulate my mood, and have fun."

When Roy opened his academy, he had to change targets by making the shift from employee to entrepreneur.

"It's a mental shift as much as a business shift," Roy said. "I used to be more focused on becoming famous and making money. You have to get into this space of a prosperity mind-set, and that is a useful tool. But it's not an end in itself."

Roy has known many wealthy people and has seen their initial thrill of making money, but once they get used to it, making more money creates no emotion at all.

"How much is enough?" Roy asked. "It's just like competition. That's an endless world that you can get sucked into. In terms of prosperity, I feel very grateful that I'm able to do what I do. I lead a comfortable life, but I'm not deeply obsessed with getting rich. I don't want to be the richest man in the graveyard."

Today, Roy's focus is on creating art through Jiu-Jitsu media that inspires people from a technical standpoint but is also entertaining and pleasing to the eye.

"I feel very fortunate that I was exposed to Jiu-Jitsu at a young age," Roy said. "Today, I feel that I've turned the corner, because traditionally the warrior's journey is warrior, teacher, healer. I haven't done the healing arts yet, but I'm investing in the next generation to help them save a few steps along the way, as my teacher did for me."

Ryron Gracie

At 12 years old, Ryron Gracie cleaned the mats in between matches at UFC 1 where Royce Gracie submitted every one of his opponents.

That event changed history and radically transformed the martial arts community. UFC 1 showcased Gracie Jiu-Jitsu to the world and planted the seeds for Brazilian Jiu-Jitsu to spread internationally.

"I had a pretty good idea how big the UFC was," Ryron said. "Everybody at my school knew I was there and that my uncle was on TV."

Twenty-five years later, Ryron is routinely recognized by people who are anxious to share their story of watching the early UFC fights.

"But it's not about me," Ryron emphasized. "It's the name. Torrance is very much the city of the Gracie family."

Ryron grew up in Torrance, California, where his father, Rorion Gracie, founded the Gracie Jiu-Jitsu Academy. Today, Ryron and his brother, Rener, invest their time and energy in Gracie University, where they continue to teach Gracie Jiu-Jitsu.

"I was in a unique place while growing up," Ryron said. "At a very young age I was surrounded by my father, uncles, and grandfather, all of whom other men admired. They became my heroes after I saw how much people respected my elders. I wanted that, so I followed my family."

In adolescence, most kids rebel against their parents, but Ryron spent most of his time at his father's academy.

"Most of my Jiu-Jitsu came directly from my Uncle Royce, and then my father, Rorion," Ryron said. "But the mindset on the mat and philosophy of how to actually fight came from my grandfather [Helio Gracie]."

Ryron's father wanted Ryron to attend college after high school, but to avoid school, Ryron asked to go to Brazil to learn from his grandfather.

"Don't get me wrong," Ryron said. "I didn't want to go to college, but I was excited to go to Brazil and soak up time with my grandpa, train Jiu-Jitsu, and better my Portuguese."

Ryron spent six months living with Helio. They spent every day together talking about life and training Jiu-Jitsu in the evenings on a small mat in Helio's home.

"When I got there, he really simplified my Jiu-Jitsu and opened my mind about how to behave on and off the mat," Ryron said. "Spending time with my grandfather when he was in his 80s is one of the main reasons I feel so safe when doing Jiu-Jitsu. His main objective was to teach me how to defend myself, and who better to teach me than someone his age who has been doing it for as long as he has."

In those months together, Helio shared many of his life's philosophies.

"I don't fear the rattlesnake," Helio told Ryron. "But I do respect it."

"It's the same as if you were going to fight somebody 120 pounds heavier—a monster of a man," Ryron said. "You don't fear the man, but you have to respect his size and what he is capable of."

Every day, Helio prepared them a healthy breakfast.

"My grandfather gives a lot of credit to food," Ryron said. "What you eat and drink can determine how you will live, so he woke up every morning at 5:30 and made us an amazing fruit smoothie."

At 86, Helio was spontaneous and sometimes drove to the city to bring Ryron to the local Jiu-Jitsu schools to train.

"I watched my grandfather walking down the street in Brazil getting stopped many times," Ryron said. "A 60-plus-year-old man walked up to my 85-year-old grandfather and said, 'My father took me to watch your fight when I was a child. It was an honor to watch you. I can't believe I'm seeing you here in person.'"

The UFC brought Helio back into the limelight with the Brazilian youth, but it was the older generations who had seen his fights in person, and Helio always made time to talk to them and make them feel special.

"Lots of people out there know his story," Ryron said. "Helio was Brazil's first national sports hero."

Ryron returned to the U.S. and began teaching full time at the Gracie Jiu-Jitsu Academy. He taught every morning and noon class, and his brother, Rener, helped teach the evening classes after high school let out.

At age 21, Ryron was awarded his black belt from Grand Master Helio Gracie. At that age, Ryron's perspective of life and success was very different than it is today.

"I don't really think success was on my mind back then," Ryron said. "I just wanted to do what my family was known for— teaching Jiu-Jitsu."

But like a lot of young people, Ryron also wanted to make money to buy things and have fun.

"I think people chase money because it feels good," Ryron said. "It feels like you're winning to see your income go up. It can be part of your self-worth."

Years later, Ryron has a very different point of view.

"Today, with two children, in many ways, success is raising them," Ryron said. "Having children has really simplified my life. Once you have a wife, kids, and a home, there are more things that require your attention, so it really becomes important to find balance, and balance doesn't mean equal time for each piece of the pie. It just means giving each piece what it needs. I understand that now, and it's not easy."

Finding balance required Ryron to do more than prioritize his time.

"More than ever, success is being able to live very simply," Ryron said. "Not necessarily having enough money to own six cars or fly first-class, but having just enough to live, eat well, and have a comfortable roof over my head."

Ryron is a lot more aware of how he spends money, and today he's living conservatively and planning for many years into the future.

"I do the same thing I do when I train Jiu-Jitsu," Ryron said. "I want to be able to train for the next 40 years, so I don't go out there and beat everybody up in a two-minute roll. I am practicing being a 70-year-old today by rolling slowly with lots of control, weight, and patience. I'm behaving the way I will need to in order to continue playing this game when I'm 70."

Ryron used to do 30 private Jiu-Jitsu lessons per week and had 30 students on a waiting list.

"It became too much," Ryron said. "I had to pace myself because Jiu-Jitsu is very demanding on our bodies. I've changed how I approach each roll. I'm not trying to prove that I'm the best every time I roll. I don't need to prove it every day."

Ryron does not mind letting the new guy, or even an experienced black belt, submit him. His students are there because of his ability to share what he knows, not because he can tap them out.

"It's all about their energy," Ryron said. "If I roll with a black belt and there is a good back-and-forth energy, they just want to flow. They're not in this proving mode and they don't care to beat me as much as they care to experience me. That's different than if they're rolling hard and want to beat me."

Ryron said the ego is a confusing thing because it has a strong presence in everything we do.

"Even when I decide to play with my kids and not be on my phone, it's my ego that makes me strive to be super dad," Ryron said. "I just try to manipulate the ego in a way that best serves my goals in life."

Ryron explained that many children are raised to believe their self-esteem is measured by their accomplishments.

"Maybe they were raised in a household where they got their sense of self-worth from winning a trophy or a better report card," Ryron said. "Now as adults they continue that, and work is one way they can win, so they strive for validation through their career."

When Ryron and his wife had their first child, they did a home birth, and Ryron did not leave the house for about 10 days.

"As a young father, going to work felt like going on a vacation," Ryron said. "I had a wife and a child at home who I love very much, but I felt like I was drowning at home. I remember justifying that I needed to make money to buy my family nice things, but I needed a way out. When I went to work, I felt like I was in Hawaii."

Ryron explained how exhausting and stressful it is having young children.

"I can only imagine how my wife felt," Ryron said. "When you have children, you're back at zero, starting as a beginner. You're in this place where at home you have no idea what to do with a two-month-old, but in your work, even though there are struggles, it's your game—you've been working there for a long time."

Ryron said he can see why a father might want to escape back to work because it's where they feel most effective.

"People tend to go where they're comfortable," Ryron said. "In Jiu-Jitsu we say you want to hang out in the uncomfortable to make it to where uncomfortable positions cease to exist."

Ryron was raised to thrive in discomfort. When Ryron was 18 years old, his grandfather forced him to spend months allowing every one of his training partners to have the top position.

"I was not a big fan of people being on top of me when I was fighting," Ryron said. "After a whole year of it I was frustrated. I didn't understand it."

Months later, Ryron was fighting a guy who got the top position that would have previously been a serious threat.

"It was no problem," Ryron said. "Right then the lightbulb went off. My grandfather gave me the gift of comfort underneath anybody for the rest of my life."

Ryron said that just like in Jiu-Jitsu, in business, people have a plan because they cannot afford not to.

"But at home, it's trial and error," Ryron said. "When it comes to parenting, if you do not have a plan, before you know it, you've missed the opportunities to give your kids the lessons they need to make decisions that are going to help them throughout life."

Ryron has grown to share his wife's belief that we can learn volumes from our children, which has taught him to appreciate the challenges of parenting.

"Learning these things from my wife has allowed me to feel equally rewarded staying at home with my children," Ryron said. "Now when I stay home, I get a whole day to learn while I engage with them."

Getting to that place as a parent required the same steps it takes to excel in Jiu-Jitsu and anything else.

"First you must acknowledge your discomfort," Ryron said. "You have to be aware of where you're uncomfortable and live in that moment."

As Ryron grew as a father, the desire to escape the home decreased.

"I no longer feel like I'm not growing in my business, because instead, I'm growing at home," Ryron said. "I still make money; I just stopped some of the things that are not giving me the most return. It's important to know where to invest your time—and don't spend a lot of time doing things that are not giving you the most return. And right now, with my kids being so young, I'm focused on growing my family currency."

Ryron described how easy it is for busy parents to use the phone to bring their work home. With all the modern distractions, it's easy to become impatient when kids compete for their parents' attention.

"I've had to compromise, because if it's in my pocket beeping every few minutes … ," Ryron said and then paused. "I just make it a point to put it on the counter and be present with my children, because I know that's what we need. Playing with them with full attention for 30 minutes means a lot. Many parents don't do that because it's hard to do, but the kids notice it."

Ryron mentioned the tug-of-war of family life that competes for time with his business. Both his family and business depend on him, but he depends on his family and business as well.

"I feel that success is finding balance," Ryron said of all the things competing for his time. "Success is giving time to my wife to maintain the marriage, but also giving time to myself. And raising the children to become self-sufficient while also doing what I love and generating income."

Ryron mentioned that we work hard for most of our lives. As kids, we are in school from ages 6 to 18, and then we go to work until we are about 70.

"They're pitching this idea of retiring at 70 years old, which is crazy," Ryron said. "I feel like at 70 you can't even retire anymore. I want to be able to do yoga, kayaking, mountain biking, and go see the world."

Ryron explained that teaching Jiu-Jitsu is very rewarding, but it's taxing on the mind and body. Although Jiu-Jitsu does not feel like work, there will come a time when he will need to cut back, and hopefully that will come before he is 70.

Ryron is working to create passive streams of income through Jiu-Jitsu. The growth of their programs enables them to expand the reach of Gracie Jiu-Jitsu much further than he could through private and group Jiu-Jitsu lessons, while also providing a healthier family/work balance.

"We're sharing something very valuable, and nobody else shares it like we do," Ryron said. "It feels great to give what we're giving on a larger scale."

The transformation Ryron gets to experience from their students is what motivates him. Ryron described a student who was 70 pounds overweight, afraid to go to school, and would not make eye contact with people.

"How many kids were bullied, or grew up without much of a male presence, and then become adults who do not have much confidence?" Ryron said. "Jiu-Jitsu is for everyone—the student, the type-A attorney, the bank clerk, and the mailman."

Ryron said that part of the job of the male instructors is to provide some of the masculine energy that many people do not get to experience while growing up.

"Fighting is good for men and women, but it can be a very macho thing," Ryron said. "The ability to defend yourself does a lot of healing. After three to six months, we begin to see them break free from these agreements they've made with themselves. It's almost like they've agreed they're weak, powerless, incapable, or whatever. Jiu-Jitsu is an injection of confidence. Jiu-Jitsu is medicine."

Ryron said simply watching his students begin to stand up straight, hold a conversation, and make eye contact is very rewarding.

"That's what drives us," Ryron said. "Even though I'm going to work, it's not work. It's very rewarding."

Ryron explained that if he were to inherit $40 million tomorrow, he would not stop teaching Jiu-Jitsu.

"The energy is too special around this," Ryron said. "That energy is worth something. Even when I retire, I want to show up three or four times a week just to share my experience and soak in the energy that exists in the building. So, I guess that means I won't be retiring."

In many ways, according to Ryron, he has two wives.

"My wife makes me feel very special," Ryron said. "She loves and cares for me, but so does my other wife—Jiu-Jitsu. It still gives me so much. Jiu-Jitsu will be here forever."

Gracie Jiu-Jitsu is Ryron's family, and it has been there his entire life.

"My grandfather is responsible for that," Ryron said. "His name is my name, so every Gracie who is out there is fighting to push the Gracie name forward because it's tied to something so special."

Recently, while Ryron was walking in Beverly Hills, a man approached him to introduce himself and his friend.

"You're standing in front of a legend," the older man told his friend about Ryron.

"He's not saying that because I'm a legend," Ryron said. "It's bigger than me. Gracie Jiu-Jitsu started with Helio and Carlos Gracie. What he's saying is that you're in front of 70 years of fighting history. I'm just one guy on the street in flip-flops, but he's counting everything combined and giving me that credit. I'm just a messenger."

Ryron is more concerned about promoting Gracie Jiu-Jitsu than self-promotion.

"That's all I know. There is no me," Ryron said. "I might win a Jiu-Jitsu match, but not for me. It's more to prove the effectiveness of Jiu-Jitsu like everybody else before me has."

Ryron attempts to deflect attention from himself but admits it's hard to ignore the power and respect that come from being part of a legendary family of fighters.

Helio told Ryron there are three forms of power in the world: the media, money, and physical power.

"If you control the media, or have billions of dollars, you're one of the most powerful people in the world," Ryron said. "But if you put me in the room with that billionaire, even with all of his money, he is very aware of the physical imbalance, and there is power in that."

Ryron explained that people gravitate to that type of power, which is why powerful people from all walks of life make their way to Jiu-Jitsu schools to associate with martial artists and fighters. Power attracts power.

"I don't have the liquid wealth that these people have, but I have a wealth of Jiu-Jitsu, and that has a lot of value," Ryron said.

There is a lot of responsibility that comes with the power of being a Gracie Jiu-Jitsu black belt.

"I don't call it humble as much as I call it a very clear definition as to what ego is," Ryron said. "The more confident I have become, the more in control or aware I am of my ego. Because I am so well prepared for physical confrontation, my ego is less confrontational. I feel less of a need to prove myself. The ego is everywhere. It is a beautiful thing, but most people don't talk about it enough to even understand it."

Ryron explained that the word ego has a negative connotation, but if people talked about it, they would be more open to understanding how the ego drives us.

"When people get mad or argue about something, it's usually about something deeper," Ryron said. "I'm at the point where no matter what anybody says, I try to have empathy for that person. Everything is filtered through their life experiences and cultural backgrounds and then projected onto me. Nothing is personal."

Helio had shared his philosophy that if someone were to attack his daughter and then run away, Helio would not hunt the guy down to retaliate.

"If I'm there and he comes to the house, that's different. He's got to go through me," Helio told Ryron. "But if I weren't there, it's already done, and he's gone. It's in the past. It doesn't matter."

Years later Ryron read two inspirational books: *The Four Agreements* and *The Power of Now*.

"Years later when I was reading those books, my grandfather had already passed away," Ryron said. "I was realizing that there are just so many things he said that are in those books. He was ahead of his time."

Ryron kept thinking about *The Power of Now* and how it relates to Jiu-Jitsu.

"When people are fighting the take-down, for example, after they get taken down they continue to fight as if they were still on their feet," Ryron said. "You fight on your feet because you don't want to go down, but once you go down you have to become immediately present to the new position."

Ryron said the two most common mistakes in all of Jiu-Jitsu are trying to escape too soon and trying to attack or advance too early.

"This tells us that people are uncomfortable in both the inferior and superior positions in Jiu-Jitsu," Ryron said. "Ninety-five percent of failed submissions and lost positions happen because people are trying to beat their partner too early, or trying to escape the inferior position too soon. They attack too soon because they are filled with fear and want to secure victory. They rush to escape because they are afraid of an attack. Everyone is trying to be somewhere other than where they are."

Ryron said the secret to success in life, on and off the mat, is to get back to the core of Jiu-Jitsu. For example, when Ryron first gets to the mount position, the submission is the last thing on his mind.

"What's on my mind is keeping myself safe," Ryron said. "I keep myself safe by controlling them. If I'm underneath somebody, I don't want to get out. I want to make sure he can't hurt me. There's no hurry to escape."

"The path to success in life and Jiu-Jitsu is to be completely present in the position you're currently at," Ryron said, "and this is the number one challenge of my life—and I need to practice it every day."

Steve Austin

teve Austin started learning martial arts for the same reason a lot of young men do, but the pain that fueled him through overwhelming adversity was quite unique.

"I was always bullied," Steve said. "When I was a little kid, I did not realize how different I was from everyone else, but I had all these people ridiculing me. I felt like an outcast. By first or second grade, kids were already ruthless. It was not until I got a little older that I could see that something was different."

Steve was born with a hip disease called Legg-Perthes, but it was misdiagnosed when he was 3 years old. That mistake led to a rushed medical procedure, during which the surgeon passed out while abusing pharmaceutical narcotics. It was a botched surgery that Steve did not even need, and its by-product was a series of medical and emotional hardships that still affected him decades later.

During Steve's childhood, his legs were completely immobilized in a metal A-frame brace that locked his legs in the splits position.

The braces were designed to keep his hips aligned, as the disease deteriorated his hips.

Many years later, the boy with steel braces on his legs became the Brazilian Jiu-Jitsu black belt with a vise-grip-like guard. Steve is the founder of Sion BJJ in Southampton, Pennsylvania. He is an active competitor in matches that include Metamoris Challenger and Fight 2 Win. In addition to teaching the public, he also trains police officers, celebrity clients, and Hollywood movie fight choreographers.

Steve began training in Jiu-Jitsu almost two decades ago, but he has been fighting since he was very young.

"The first time I had to defend myself was in second grade, after a kid was making fun of me for still wearing diapers," Steve said. "A side effect of the botched surgery was that my bowel was cut in half. At seven years old, I still had to wear a diaper to school, so kids wondered what the hell was the matter. I got made fun of a lot for that."

After three years in the leg braces, he was able to slowly transition out of them.

"I wasn't allowed to walk around," Steve explained. "I had to be in a wheelchair or use a walker because my legs were kind of like jello. They never really developed during my childhood because I had to crawl around using my arms."

Steve's legs weakened so much while he was in leg braces that he constantly got injured from the slightest fall.

"I wanted to be a normal kid and play sports," Steve said. "But I wasn't allowed to play contact sports, so I would run track, do bowling, or anything, but I'd get hurt doing stupid stuff and then I'd be out for two months."

Steve was not physically able to do the things he craved, but that did not tame his desire to do so.

"I grew up watching all the ninja and action movies," Steve said. "I ran around the house with an elastic bandage wrapped around my head, pretending I was a ninja, and I idolized Conan and Rambo. Conan was this little kid who had his childhood stolen, but he trained and came back a ruthless fighter—ah, man, I wanted to grow up to be like that."

Steve begged his mother to let him try martial arts, but she was worried about the risks.

"Of course, she said no," Steve said, "and I realized I might never get that chance."

As Steve grappled with normal teenage stress on top of his medical problems, he struggled to find a place where he belonged.

"I went through all these different phases trying to find where I fit in," Steve said. "I tried different styles—goth, industrial, skater—and dyed my hair blue. I got made fun of for that, but I didn't really care because at least I had control over that, and it took the attention away from my medical issues."

While playing basketball, Steve was tripped; he injured his knee and broke his foot, but because the hip disease had caused nerve damage, he had limited feeling in his leg.

"I walked on a broken foot for weeks before realizing it was injured," Steve said. "Three months after surgery, I remember getting into a fight with a kid I didn't even know, because he teased me for walking with a limp. I was an easy target and getting picked on a lot, so I really needed to learn how to defend myself."

As Steve entered his teenage years, he kept getting into fights and asked his mother if he could learn tae kwon do. This time she reluctantly agreed, and he started progressing through the belt ranks.

"I was 15 when things were starting to come together for me," Steve said. "I had a girlfriend, a lot of friends, and I was hanging out and having fun until suddenly it was all ripped away from me."

The knee he previously had surgery on began causing problems again. He returned to a doctor, who recommended another surgery.

"I just heard the word 'brace,'" Steve said. "Fuck, I just about lost it. It felt like PTSD or something, and it set me back mentally. I wanted to do all these things, but I've got to go through this again?! It was that second knee surgery at 16 that really sent me down a bad path. Sixteen to 18 were not good years for me physically or emotionally."

That second knee surgery was the catalyst that ultimately drove Steve to a dark place and caused him to be institutionalized.

"Puberty is a motherfucker, and I just couldn't handle it anymore," Steve said. "You're at the peak of your testosterone, and I had all these issues holding me back. Then I found out that I was a product of an affair. My dad didn't want much to do with me, so I never had that male role model to teach me to suck it up and be a man. It was very difficult feeling unwanted by my own father. It was just a lot of things, and I reached a point that I had a mental breakdown."

Following surgery, Steve was prescribed narcotic painkillers, which he realized would numb him from feeling any emotional pain.

"I didn't really care about anything when that stuff was in my system," Steve said. "I was introduced to really hard drugs, and I was getting high as hell. I lost the ability to care about myself or my life, and I probably made my knee worse because I didn't want to wear the brace or use crutches. I wanted to be back to normal as fast as possible. I rushed the recovery and hurt myself a couple times over-doing it, but I didn't give a shit."

When everything collided in adolescence, it was like mixing baking soda and vinegar, and Steve became reckless.

"I didn't care, because there was nothing anyone could do to hurt me more than I had already been hurt. I almost felt invincible, but when I looked ahead, it scared the shit out of me because it felt hopeless."

While taking drugs, Steve cut his wrists and later accidentally overdosed on ketamine, an animal anesthetic referred to as Special K when used recreationally.

"I went through a phase where I just didn't feel any pain," Steve said. "I was so used to pain, but I would wonder why things stopped hurting me."

Steve had a bad reaction to ketamine, collapsed to the floor in the middle of science class, and was rushed to the hospital.

"It's very emotional even bringing this up now," Steve said. "That overdose was a wake-up call. I didn't really have a grip on what was happening, but I remember being rushed to the hospital and feeling like I was slipping into the abyss. I was trying not to let go, because I really wanted to stay alive.

"It was almost like the scene at the end of the Rambo movie, *First Blood*. I was so angry, but it was all bottled up, and then I just exploded in anger. After going through that meltdown, I felt my life being taken away from me, and I was scared."

After the hospital, Steve was sent to counselors, who attempted to help.

"It was scary because I had to tell them everything that had been going on in my head," Steve said. "I was dealing with a lifelong battle of health issues, and nobody could relate. Everyone treated me like shit because of it, and I just wanted to know why. All they could say was, 'I don't know what to tell you, man. I'm sorry. God works in mysterious ways.'

"I joke that what does not kill you just puts you in the hospital. There are a lot of people used to having it easy, and when they finally face a challenge and fail, they break because they don't know how to handle it. You have to build mental toughness to survive life."

The hospital visit was Steve's wake-up call, but what really turned his life around was when his girlfriend got pregnant.

"I was only 19, so it was not planned whatsoever," Steve said. "As a matter of fact, I was completely blown away that I could even have a child. When I found out I was having a son, I decided to become a better person. I wanted to have a child who would be proud to have me as a father. I knew what it was like growing up without a dad, and I didn't want my child to go through that, and the path I was going down, I was either going to end up dead or in jail."

Steve wanted to find ways to bring positivity back into his life, so he thought of the time he was most happy. Steve remembered how much he enjoyed kempo, so he returned to martial arts. His instructor started studying Jiu-Jitsu and introduced it to the students.

"I immediately fell in love," Steve said. "When I went through the ranks in kempo, I started seeing some mystical hooky kind of bullshit. I've been in a lot of fights, and I'm never going to get into a fuckin' cat's stance. But in Jiu-Jitsu, I got my ass handed to me. I had gotten the worst of it in some fights, but I never got manhandled in a fight like that I did in Jiu-Jitsu.

Steve technically started Jiu-Jitsu at 19 years old, but he said he had been practicing it since he was 2. When he attended his first classes, he was surprised by what they were teaching.

"You've got to be kidding me," Steve said. "This is what we're doing? I was doing all these Jiu-Jitsu movements and drills since I was a kid. It's almost like I was a savant across the mat, because getting around on the ground was all I could do as a kid. It felt natural."

When people first train with Steve today, they're surprised by the strength of his guard.

"Your guard feels like you've got metal legs," his opponents have said.

"Yeah, because I wasn't able to use them the first half of my life," Steve has said. "I cannot open my legs more than an 80-degree angle, but that space is extremely well trained. It's perfect for playing guard."

The more Steve immersed himself in the sport, the happier he became.

"When I started Jiu-Jitsu, it became my center, and everything gravitated toward it to make my life better."

Jiu-Jitsu motivated Steve to stop using drugs and alcohol, and his relationships changed.

"I started to improve all my habits," Steve said. "I can't go out Friday night drinking and eating crap, because I have training in the morning. It became a reason to improve all other aspects of my life. Suddenly, I started seeing these major ripple effects, like who I surrounded myself with. I didn't need negative people in my life, and I started treating people better.

"Jiu-Jitsu gave me peace in my life because it gave me a healthy way to get my stress and aggression out. I think all men have such a buildup of testosterone and aggression, and we don't have a healthy way to release it. We're like a steam kettle: You've got to release some pressure or it's going to blow."

Steve explained how men in modern society lack a rite of passage.

"We no longer have a test of manhood," Steve said. "As a matter of fact, we're almost pussifying everyone now. I feel like the blue belt is your first rite of passage into manhood because you've got your ass kicked for about two years. You could have easily quit, but you decided to continue to suffer because there's a reward at the end. For most people, blue belt will be the hardest thing they've ever done because you're going to fail over and over, but you continue to persevere through failure and start to come out on top a little."

This growth process becomes addicting for many reasons, some of which are explained by science. Steve described the chemicals that flow through our body—endorphins, dopamine, oxytocin, and serotonin, which affect how we feel. Humans get endorphins from exercise. Today most people get dopamine from unhealthy addictions like social media. We get a rush of serotonin from positive feedback and oxytocin from interaction with others. Jiu-Jitsu is addicting because we receive all these benefits while training.

"When they're out of balance, it's a recipe for disaster," Steve said. "But let's face it, oxytocin is really what addicts me to Jiu-Jitsu. There's a camaraderie in Jiu-Jitsu unlike in any other atmosphere. The only thing I've seen that is somewhat similar is the military.

"We're going through this journey with each other that's dangerous, experimental, extremely difficult, but so rewarding. Somebody that doesn't do Jiu-Jitsu has no idea how many years you've gotten busted up and broken on the mat or how many times you've gone home to ice, take ibuprofen, and grab a bottle of rum."

Having Jiu-Jitsu as an outlet has helped Steve find acceptance.

"I had to accept my life for what it was," Steve said. "I was angry for years and blaming people for doing me wrong. I was playing victim and holding onto resentment. I was a victim of that doctor. I was a victim of my dad. I was a victim of people bullying me. I was that dog that was just poked and backed into a corner for so long that anytime somebody walked by, I would just growl, 'Stay the fuck away.' I was always in fight mode."

Steve told the Cherokee tale of the two wolves that live inside of us. One is bad, one is good, but both are hungry; which one will you feed?

"I was fueled by anger," Steve said. "I was holding onto things—plotting out revenge against that doctor, and I visualized the day I met my dad and just punched him in the mouth. They were all negative, and the more I fed that wolf, the more life sucked."

Steve described a dog with three legs that does not go through life depressed. It wakes up, eats, and is usually happy.

"As humans, we start to feel sorry for ourselves," Steve said. "We limit what we're capable of because we feel shame, guilt, and depressed about our situation. It's this awful spiral where it infects everything in our lives."

Jiu-Jitsu gave Steve strength, not just physically but mentally.

"I realized that not only can I defend myself, but I can beat most people if I have to," Steve said. "I was no longer weak, nor was I weak-minded. I started noticing little changes, like smiling about things instead of getting pissed off and punching a hole in the wall.

"When I was younger, if somebody made fun of me, I would get angry and go into fight mode. I was insecure and felt like I had to defend myself. Today, I can talk about something because I know 100 percent that if it came down to me having to defend myself, you're going to regret it."

"I don't want to fight by any means," Steve said. "Now I can defend myself and I have the confidence that I don't feel like I have anything to prove. If people really want to fight me, I give them business cards and invite them to the gym, and they kind of think twice. Verbal Jiu-Jitsu is one of the coolest side effects of Brazilian Jiu-Jitsu."

Jiu-Jitsu taught Steve what success really means.

"Most people look at failure as trying something and not getting the outcome you were looking for," Steve said. "To me, failure is the moment I try something, it doesn't work, and then I quit trying. That's true failure in my eyes."

When an instructor teaches a new technique, it takes students repeated failed attempts before it begins to work.

"Were those hundreds of times that I did not get the outcome I was looking for, a failure?" Steve asked. "To me, it's just part of the learning process. You must learn to thrive and grow in failure because that's the only way you're going to succeed."

Tom DeBlass

Tom DeBlass stood across the octagon from his opponent moments before his last mixed martial arts fight began.

"My mindset going into every fight was to destroy the object in front of me," Tom said. "I didn't really look at them as human beings. I looked at them as objects that were physically trying to impose their will on me, so I wanted to execute my will against them."

The fighters had traded strikes for 93 seconds into the first round when Tom connected with a tight left hook. His opponent dropped to the ground but immediately popped back up, and the fight continued. Only 13 seconds later, Tom landed the same left hook, and the fight was over.

That is the moment when most fighters explode with excitement to celebrate their moment of glory, but Tom dropped to his knees to embrace the other fighter, who was unconscious on the mat.

"The moment I knocked him out, I questioned what I was doing there," Tom said. "It was hard to celebrate when I knew he also had a daughter and his whole world had just come crashing down."

Hurting opponents was never Tom's goal, but to win in MMA, you have to hurt the other person; otherwise, that person is going to hurt you.

"It was just a weird feeling," Tom said. "For sure, I want to be the one winning, but another person had to lose viciously. That's when I knew my run was coming to an end with this MMA thing."

* * *

Tom DeBlass is a UFC veteran with a professional mixed martial arts record of nine wins and two losses. Tom is a third-degree black belt under Ricardo Almeida and is a world champion Jiu-Jitsu competitor with numerous championship wins at ADCC, No Gi Worlds, Grappler's Quest, and others. He is the founder of Ocean County Jiu-Jitsu in New Jersey and has created numerous BJJ instructional videos for BJJ Fanatics.

Tom's drive, which has enabled him to become one of the top American Jiu-Jitsu competitors, began when he was young.

"My story is pretty deep," Tom said. "What led me to become successful has been a lot of pain and suffering. I've been through things most humans have not been through—emotionally, I suffered a lot."

Tom described his dad as a loving father, but he struggled with drugs and alcohol when Tom was growing up.

"I saw a lot as a kid," Tom said. "Seeing some of the things I went through was not always easy. I had to overcome a lot of emotional hardship and sadness, but I wouldn't take back a thing. Everything I went through made me who I am today. It's made me unbreakable. It's given me extreme resilience and perseverance because I've already seen so much, so what else can be thrown at me that I can't handle?"

Tom was an aggressive kid, so at 19, he found Brazilian Jiu-Jitsu, which gave him a positive outlet.

"I had a lot of anger," Tom said, "but I never used that aggression to hurt innocent people. I always wanted to fight for a cause, so I found Jiu-Jitsu."

When Tom began Jiu-Jitsu, he was driven by his need to win, and it was resilience that enabled him to become successful.

"Some people break mentally," Tom said. "If you're not willing to come back day after day, regardless of how you feel, you're never going to make it. Pressure cracks people, and a lot of people break when the pressure comes on. You can't just walk away when things are tough. You've got to fight through your toughest days."

That resilience has enabled Tom to become very successful in Jiu-Jitsu and MMA, but the appeal of medals was short-lived.

"As soon as I won, I wanted to win more," Tom said. "It was immediate gratification, but then it was empty because I was never satisfied."

Tom still enjoys competition, but looking back, he would have done it a little differently.

"The one thing I would have changed," Tom said, "is I would have been happier with my accomplishments rather than just looking for the next one. I still enjoy competing and being a champion, but I've also learned the most important things in life are not medals. The most important thing in life is helping others.

"Even though I've been through a lot, I never resented the human race because of it. It made me compassionate to other people who were suffering. It made me want to help them. I realized I could touch people's lives emotionally through Jiu-Jitsu and help them change their life for the better."

Tom saw the potential of Jiu-Jitsu to help people lose weight, relieve stress, and reach their personal goals.

"I'm working on touching as many lives as possible," Tom said. "It was such an inspiration for me to reach a level where I could inspire other people to overcome some of the obstacles I overcame. How can I not wake up inspired every day when I have the ability to change people's lives?"

Chuck Rylant

About the author written by Cindy Cyr

Growing up, Chuck Rylant was driven to become a real-life hero. Not having a healthy father figure in his life, Chuck sought out male role models, which ultimately came through the fictional characters he saw in movies. He was naturally drawn to action movie heroes of the eighties such as Sylvester Stallone in *Rambo*, Bruce Willis in *Die Hard*, and Mel Gibson in *Lethal Weapon*, and these heroes were his inspiration throughout a traumatic childhood that was filled with chaos.

In and out of foster homes when he was young, Chuck grew up on welfare and in government housing projects from the time he was born until he was 16, at which point he moved out to live on his own.

His mom suffered from severe mental illness. When she was on medication, she was loving and somewhat of a savant at math. "She was just like the character in that movie, *A Beautiful Mind*," Chuck explained. His most cherished memory of his mom is when she would help him with his math, something he had hated until he had his own son and realized the incredible patience she displayed while teaching. But most of his memories of his mom involve mental health professionals, the police, and child protective services.

"I remember coming home one day and noticing the big dumpster at our housing project was full of furniture," Chuck recalled. "I recognized some of it and was confused. I didn't know what was happening. I went inside, and our entire house was empty. Everything was in the trash. I don't really have any family photos because they were all thrown away during that time."

"I remember the police showing up," Chuck continued. "And being interviewed by child protective services. I used to try so hard to be normal, so every time these government people would be involved, I would say everything was great. I would tell them I didn't need their help. I really did need something, but I'd fake it and pretend that I was normal."

It turned out that Chuck's mom was having a mental breakdown. She was taken away. His dad wasn't involved much, and the furniture was never replaced.

Chuck's father never worked and didn't participate much as a father. "He was a deadbeat with lots of issues stemming from childhood trauma," Chuck said. "He was selfish, angry, and violent, and he suffered from extreme depression and OCD."

A fanatical Christian, his father walked around town with a large wooden cross. "Everybody knew it was my father, and they would constantly bring it up," Chuck said. "The first time he walked around with the cross, I was so upset. I lost my mind and asked him, 'Why would you do this? Why are you so selfish? Why don't you think about the impact this will have on us?' While that was going on, a group of kids knocked on the door and made a comment about my dad and punched me in the stomach while I was standing in the doorway. It was completely unprovoked. I can't even explain to this day why somebody would be so bothered they'd come to physically attack me."

"I was so ashamed of my life," Chuck continued. "My mom was odd with her mental illness. My dad was odd with his religion ... but that was the abnormal weird stuff. Then I had the normal embarrassing stuff. I was poor. We lived in a housing project. I was on welfare and food stamps. None of my clothes fit because they were worn-out hand-me-down clothes. I was very much ashamed that neither of my parents ever worked. I had to live with these embarrassing things, but I didn't know how to explain it. I still don't know how to today. My desire to be normal was so powerful that I tried to hide the shame I lived with each day, so anytime someone tried to intervene, I would pretend to be normal and dismiss it."

Even at a young age, he understood that his family didn't have enough money for even the basics such as clothes, let alone fun stuff like toys. Chuck knew he would have to learn how to make it on his own. This motivated him to work any chance he got—everything from a newspaper route to selling door-to-door to pulling weeds and mowing lawns to construction.

"I remember being a real pain in the ass to anyone who was doing labor around town," Chuck recalled. "It was not uncommon for me to hang around a construction site and watch what they were doing. Then I'd just start picking up wood and carrying it ... whatever it was they were doing, I'd just jump in and start doing it. I was probably 12. This happened so often that I guess I was doing the right thing because no one ever chased me away, and often they'd throw me some money. Sometimes they'd say come back tomorrow."

"I had a worker's permit when I was 14," Chuck recalled. "My first real job, I would swing a pickaxe in the sun for eight hours a day, breaking up dirt. The guy who started with me quit after a few days, but I was happy because I made a real paycheck all summer, and I bought some nice clothes for school the following year. I was feeling very confident having earned those nice clothes. That pattern of hard work, reward, then feeling good about myself, it just kept repeating. So I've never not worked, and I continue to have this mind-set today ... I think it came from not having enough."

Looking back on things, Chuck realized that to keep kids from making fun of him, he rebelled against authority figures by trying to make them the "common enemy." This pushed adults away, which reinforced the label he felt both adults and kids had given him because of his parents. He was never a bully to other kids, but he was a tyrant in school.

"Looking back, I think my subconscious thought was that if I was on the offense, either by being class clown and making them laugh, or by being in this constant battle with the teachers who I saw as the enemy, I assumed kids would not mess with me."

In high school, Chuck continued his rebellious streak, which caused adults to judge him. Some of it was deserved, but even those who did not know him would make derogatory comments too. This fueled Chuck to work harder to prove people wrong.

"I felt superior to anyone in authority. Parents, teachers, and so on. I think that came from being the 'adult' among mentally ill parents in my house," Chuck said.

"I felt everyone else painted me in this picture as a person who I was not," Chuck said. "I consciously started sculpting who I was going to become and doing things to make that person real. I was a skinny, scrawny kid, so I started lifting weights. I was intimidated and didn't know how to fight, so I learned how to fight. It was all very intentional. I didn't want to be the person I was, so I decided to create my character and become the man I wanted to be."

Turning to his movie-hero influences for guidance, Chuck watched Steven Seagal movies and tried to reverse engineer the fake moves he saw on TV at home. "I wanted to be fearless," Chuck said. "I wanted to be able to protect myself and protect weak people." Proactively seeking out how to fight, at 14, Chuck found someone willing to take him to the YMCA, where he got his first martial arts training. This became an outlet for his anger. "It was all adults and me," Chuck said. "I was fighting these men and doing pretty well." At about the same time, he also joined a police explorer program.

Despite his work ethic and channeling his anger through Tae Kwon Do, life could have taken a very different turn for Chuck at this point. Fortunately, an influential high school teacher named Jeff Jeffries appeared and took Chuck under his wing. Jeff ran the agriculture program and gave Chuck odd jobs such as pulling weeds, and later a real job doing welding and repairs, which Chuck worked at after school.

"I think I would have been a drug dealer if it wasn't for Jeff," Chuck said. "There were a lot of drugs around and a guy who would hang around the school who always carried a gun and would pull out wads of cash. I thought it was so cool that he had a gun and cash. He started taking me around on drug deals and kind of mentoring me. But Jeff would keep me busy and tell me, 'Get away from those guys, I've got work for you to do.'"

Jeff got Chuck involved with a program called Future Farmers of America (FFA). Chuck was excelling in welding and other competitions, and it was there that he experienced his first measurable achievement, when the three-person FFA team he was on won the state level competition and advanced to nationals. Chuck also took 3rd in the state.

After finishing high school early, Chuck worked full time while attending community college. Undecided on his future, he worked at an auto shop and took classes to become an auto mechanic while earning an AA degree in hopes of becoming a stockbroker. After finishing his two-year degree, he applied to Cal Poly University, where he was accepted for an economics major.

Two factors influenced his decision to turn down Cal Poly and instead follow his friends from the police explorer program and pay his way through the police academy. First, he thought it would be easier to save up six months of living expenses than to save for four years of college. Second, there were the heroes who had influenced his thinking his entire life.

"Sylvester Stallone's characters were my primary influence," Chuck said. "I'm naturally inclined to believe in right and wrong. I don't know where that comes from; it's just who I am. I'm really sympathetic to the underdog, and I want to protect that person. I don't like bullies. So the whole idea of police officers protecting people seemed like a natural fit. But the main reason I became a cop was for the action. I wanted to do car chases. I wanted to get in fights. I wanted to be the hero. I wanted to be admired, looked up to, and respected. In the early years that was the drive."

It was also during this time following high school that Chuck began competing in Tae Kwon Do. In his first fight, at just 18 years of age, he used his best combination—a roundhouse kick to the ribs immediately followed by a second kick to the head. He knocked his opponent out cold in just ten seconds, winning his first match.

"I felt completely dominant in that moment," Chuck said. "It was invigorating, and that confidence spilled over into my future matches. I don't think I ever lost a Tae Kwon Do tournament, and I brought that feeling of invincibility into my law enforcement career."

Chuck's anger and ambition to prove people wrong hadn't left him at this point, making this his main driving factor. Only this time, the discipline he'd learned through Tae Kwon Do drove him to succeed rather than to be defiant.

"In the early days, the police academy was very intimidating to me," Chuck recalled. "It's just like you'd see with the military drill sergeant in the movies, but that didn't intimidate me as much as failing. I was petrified of failing because I felt this was my only option. I remember being in the formation where you stand still at attention with your arms at your side and you look straight ahead. The guy has the Smokey Bear hat with a brim and he gets in your face and screams at you. He's spitting at you and belittling you. And I remember my internal dialogue while looking at this guy. I told myself, 'I will allow him to continue talking to me this way because I'm choosing not to beat his ass.' At least in my mind, this shifted the power curve to where I was in control of the whole environment."

Later, Chuck would discover that his composure and internal dialogue set him apart. "At the end of the academy, when they wrote a report about us, this extremely intimidating drill sergeant wrote, 'Mr. Rylant has this unusual aura of confidence about him, unlike any other recruit I've ever seen. Nothing seems to faze him.'"

Chuck graduated valedictorian, receiving almost every other award from the police academy too. People began noticing what he had been trying to prove all along, and this instilled pride and fueled more success. He began working patrol, eventually becoming a trainer to new officers, teaching them about firearms and fighting.

"I got really confident because I started knocking people out at tournaments," Chuck said. "I was becoming bigger and lifting weights. Then I started succeeding in my career as a police officer."

In 1999, after Chuck got into a fight with a murder suspect who resisted arrest, a fellow police officer recommended he go to a Jiu-Jitsu class. "As a police officer, I got into fights all the time, but Tae Kwon Do is all kicking and punching, and you don't really kick people as a cop."

Not understanding exactly what Jiu-Jitsu was, Chuck watched a co-worker's VHS tape of the early Ultimate Fighting Championship footage of Brazilian Jiu-Jitsu fighter Royce Gracie.

"Here's this scrawny guy who's built like me. He's unassuming, and he's choking out these giant muscular bodybuilders who in the 1980s were *the* envy. Gracie beat this guy named Ken Shamrock, who looks like a Ken doll, only he's a bodybuilder. So everyone from my generation saw this as our dream. It was not the movies. It was a real-life little guy defeating the bigger man. It was a David and Goliath story. I watched these videos, and this was the most incredible thing I'd seen in my life! I was blown away. But then I thought maybe it was fake, like the WWE [World Wresting Entertainment]."

"What I saw in those UFC fights forced me to see what most of us strive to avoid—the truth," Chuck continued. "Those fights forced me to question my own abilities and challenged the validity of the martial art that had consumed a significant part of my life." Chuck showed the video to his Tae Kwon Do teacher, who told Chuck he thought the fights must be fake. Despite his teacher's take on the fights and the fact he'd invested so many years into Tae Kwon Do, Chuck reluctantly left Tae Kwon Do in his mid-twenties, choosing to train with the Gracie family instead. "I'd drive down south, three hours one way, one day a week and spend all day training," Chuck said. "I didn't realize at the time how significant it was to get to train with these people [the Gracies]."

Chuck became pretty decent at Jiu-Jitsu. He began using it, easily winning fights as a police officer. At the time Chuck started, it wasn't very common for police officers to practice and use Jiu-Jitsu. "I put some carpet pads in my garage and started inviting all my friends to train. I was kind of like the de facto teacher at the same time I was just barely learning. I just knew a little bit, but it was enough to be better than all the people I was training with."

But there was still the anger. Fighting the stigma of his parents,

Chuck married his high school sweetheart. "Her parents openly hated me because of my parents," Chuck said. "They fueled my ambition to prove them wrong. I was so angry, and I would use that anger when I was training with a punching bag or Jiu-Jitsu—I would see these people," Chuck said. "I kept working harder at life, on the mat with Jiu-Jitsu, and in the gym with weights."

Chuck proved them wrong. "I achieved all these things," Chuck said. "I owned a house, had a very successful career, had money and cars, college degrees ... all the things that to a parent, teacher, and so on looked acceptable."

But by the point they started accepting and loving him, he no longer felt he needed their approval. "I'd already proved to myself that I was successful and worthy," Chuck said.

This quickly became a problem. "I got to a point where I was arrogant," Chuck said. "At one point I started feeling not only had I made it, but now I was superior to these people. I was getting too confident. I started thinking the people who were judging me, now they were the ones who made less money or they had fewer cars or had less of a career ... I started looking down on them and thinking, 'How dare you people judge me.' That was an unhealthy period of my life."

"I was on a steady upstream, but it was all fueled by rage, hostility, anger, or a desire to prove everyone wrong," Chuck said. "That was my ammo. I was going to prove everyone wrong. I was fueled by an unhealthy motivator—by vengeance or something. And I kept pushing and pushing until I went too far."

At this point, Chuck's life started on a downward spiral. His wife cheated on him. He had business failures and setbacks in his career because of his attitude. He got injured and became dependent on prescription pain narcotics. He went through a divorce and began living an extremely unhealthy lifestyle. "A lot of bad things all happened, around the same period of my life, that really humbled me," Chuck said. "And I thought, 'Okay, you're not the badass you thought you were. You're vulnerable too.'"

Chuck also attributes part of the spiral to his idealism. "Movies were my model of the world," Chuck explained. "Meaning, there were good guys and there were bad guys. It was black and white. I was a good guy, and all the other people were bad guys. And I was so obsessed with becoming successful that my wife, my high school sweetheart, was not getting what she needed, so she ended up cheating on me. I was so naïve—I never thought that could happen to me. It totally turned my world upside down and really messed me up."

Between Chuck having issues with his mom not being there for him when he needed her and his wife cheating, he entered a very dark place where he was out of control. He hated women, but he had a need for women for sex and validation. "I had this psychotic bipolar thing going on where I would chase women and literally hate them at the same time," Chuck admitted.

During this time, he moved to a larger police department, where, just like Rambo in *First Blood*, he was confronted with the choice to walk away from a situation or "confront the bully." Chuck chose the latter, getting involved in a tumultuous political fight against a corrupt police chief. After a lengthy investigation, the chief was fired. But this was just another blow to his idealistic view of the world.

"To me, he represented the type of character in my life that I had dealt with often," Chuck said. "I had learned earlier that I would never back down from a tyrant. I would rather bring that person a war, even if it was to my own demise."

Throughout it all, Chuck was still driven to succeed, and much happened during this time. He earned his BA in business, joined the SWAT team, made detective, and started a private company on the side. Burned out on law enforcement, he followed up on his earlier passion of becoming a stockbroker. Taking a 1-year sabbatical to get his MBA from Cal Poly University, he also had a baby with his then-girlfriend. When the police department rescinded his leave of absence offer, Chuck quit. "It was the most empowering decision of my life," Chuck said.

But while things were looking up, he still had things he hadn't dealt with, and he continued through a difficult period of his life.

In 2007, one week before his MBA finals, he lost his estranged mother to cancer and his son was born and put in intensive care with a 50/50 chance of survival. "That week was brutal," Chuck recalls. "I planned my mother's funeral while sleeping in a chair at a hospital and studying for my MBA finals, and as class president, preparing a graduation keynote address."

His son recovered just in time to be present at his graduation. Following graduation, Chuck married his girlfriend, was hired back to the police force, and opened a gym business with his wife. However, after a fight with a robbery suspect left him injured, Chuck was forced out of work; and because of worker's compensation laws, he could not work in the gym business and it failed.

Out of work, in an unhealthy relationship with his wife, and coping with his injury, Chuck traveled to Brazil, where he participated in an Ayahuasca experience. Upon returning home, Chuck filed for divorce and began rebuilding his life. Only this time he went at it from a very different point of view.

"I started going to Jiu-Jitsu regularly as my body allowed," Chuck said. "And I started looking at life not as if I needed to be better than other people. I realized it's not about getting back at people. It's not about vengeance. It's about how can I be the best person I can be for myself. And in order to do that, I have to make other people's lives better, not just make myself better."

What drives Chuck these days is helping others and his desire to keep moving forward. He also makes choices for very different reasons than when he was younger.

"I don't have that emotional pain anymore," Chuck said. "I don't need to prove anything to anyone else ever again. What I'm proving to myself now is that I can keep going. That I *will* keep going."

Today, Chuck has a successful business that he loves. He coaches clients on money, business, and life. He's the author of six books. He's learned how to be in a healthy relationship with a girlfriend he's been with for five years now. He has an amazing relationship with his son, his first priority, who lives with him five to six days a week. Chuck also teaches at the police academy and does consulting for attorneys, as well as testifies as an expert witness, educating attorneys, judges, and juries in homicide trials. And he still teaches Brazilian Jiu-Jitsu and continues to work to improve himself with his most recent endeavor—working toward a PhD in psychology.

Plus, after not speaking with his father or mother for most of his life, he rekindled his relationship with his father at his mother's funeral. This allowed him to heal and have a relationship with his father before he died. "I am grateful that he was a grandfather to my son in a way that he was never a father to me," Chuck said.

Throughout all the ups and downs, one thing remained constant— Brazilian Jiu-Jitsu. It is THE superpower that, more than anything else, has changed his life and enabled him to become the hero of his story and the man he always wanted to be.

"I love Jiu-Jitsu because it's the only honest thing I have ever known," Chuck said. "The older I get, the more I realize that most of what we are told in life is not entirely true. The truth is, good grades do not equal success. The hero does not always get the pretty girl. Hard work does not always pay off. Politics prevail over skills in the workplace. Spouses cheat. Politicians lie. The list goes on and on. However, on the mat, the submission always wins. Money, good looks, sex, race, and politics do not matter on the mat. Jiu-Jitsu is honest in a world that is often dishonest. I always know where I stand on the mat. That is why I always come back."

ABOUT CINDY CYR: As a marketing consultant, strategist, and copywriter, Cindy Cyr helps companies clarify their marketing messages through stories. She's worked with clients such as Ziglar, No B.S. Inner Circle (GKIC), Dan Kennedy, Advantage | Forbesbooks, AWAI and CopyDoodles. Her clients have experienced results that include 7-Figure per year assets, increased leads, improved retention rates, doubling and tripling conversion rates and increased revenue. Learn more about Cindy at www.CincyrCopywriting.com or email her at cindy@cincyrcopywriting.com.

Before You Continue

This book is only the beginning. As a reader of this book, you are entitled to two free bonuses.

BONUS #1:

There is more available free to readers of this book at www.ChuckRylant.com. As a VIP member you will receive brand-new interviews and other inspiring articles immediately as they are published.

BONUS #2:

Readers are also eligible to receive a one-year complimentary subscription to the print newsletter **Extraordinary Living,** which is shipped via USPS to your home or office. To receive your one-year complimentary subscription visit www.ChuckRylant.com/news.

Visit www.ChuckRylant.com and
www.ChuckRylant.com/news
before you get distracted.

Books by Chuck J. Rylant

If you enjoyed this book, be sure to check out others at
www.ChuckRylant.com/amazon.

Success: *The Path to Personal Fulfillment
Through Brazilian Jiu-Jitsu Fighters*

Shots Fired: *The Psychology Behind
Officer Involved Shootings*

Motivation: *Stories on Life and Success from
Brazilian Jiu-Jitsu Black Belts*

How to be Rich: *The Small Business Owner's Guide
to Attracting Customers and Clients*

How to be Rich: *The Couple's Guide to a Rich Life
Without Worrying About Money*

Perfect Life Manifesto: *How to Achieve More This Year
Than the Past 10 Years Combined*

41138417R00082

Made in the USA
San Bernardino, CA
30 June 2019